MISSIONARY CONFERENCES

OF THE UNITED METHODIST CHURCH IN THE UNITED STATES

J. ANN CRAIG

SPECIAL CONTRIBUTOR

DEBORAH E. BASS

United Methodist Women

FAITH · HOPE · LOVE IN ACTION

Missionary Conferences of The United Methodist Church in the United States by J. Ann Craig
with contributions by Deborah E. Bass
© 2017 United Methodist Women. All rights reserved.

For all other requests, contact
Director of Transformative Education
United Methodist Women
475 Riverside Drive, Room 1501
New York, NY 10115
Phone: (212) 870-3736
Fax: (212) 870-3745

ISBN: 978-1-940182-40-7

Library of Congress Control Number: 2016958786

Art direction: Rae Grant
Cover design: Rae Grant
Cover and chapter opener image: Anson_istock
Interior design and production: Nancy Leonard

Printed in the United States of America.

United Methodist Women Purpose

The organized unit of United Methodist Women shall be a community of women whose purpose is to know God and to experience freedom as whole persons through Jesus Christ; to develop a creative, supportive fellowship; and to expand concepts of mission through participation in the global ministries of the church.

The Vision

Turning faith, hope and love into action on behalf of women, children and youth around the world.

Living the Vision

We provide opportunities and resources to grow spiritually, become more deeply rooted in Christ and put faith into action.

We are organized for growth, with flexible structures leading to effective witness and action.

We equip women and girls around the world to be leaders in communities, agencies, workplaces, governments and churches.

We work for justice through compassionate service and advocacy to change unfair policies and systems.

We provide educational experiences that lead to personal change in order to transform the world.

TABLE OF CONTENTS

FOREWORD

BY JORGE DOMINGUES

This is not a history book. It is a mission journey led by the author, J. Ann Craig, in which she guides us through the history of the missionary conferences currently in existence within The United Methodist Church—the Red Bird Missionary Conference, the Oklahoma Indian Missionary Conference, and the Alaska Conference. Acknowledging her personal connections with these conferences, the author respectfully approaches the rich and sometimes painful history of the mission engagement of The United Methodist Church and its predecessors in the context of the Appalachian Mountains, the Oklahoma Territory, and the Alaska frontier. She introduces us to the personal and collective stories of the people who have dedicated their lives to those missions and continue to lead the church in responding to God's call in those places.

These conferences are mission fields close to our hearts. They are brought to life in our communities through the faces and voices of those who have shared their stories throughout the book. They are the communities and families served by individuals, churches, and institutions that carry on the support and solidarity of United Methodist Women organized for mission with them.

The author goes beyond the missionary conferences to help us understand the connection between them and the conferences of the church that were formed on the basis of racial or ethnic identity. Through her descriptions of the experiences of the Central Jurisdiction and of the Rio Grande Conference, we hear that church structures sometimes respond to motivations that are not related to God's mission.

This study guide is a road map for the future. At a time when The United Methodist Church is taking hold of its identity as a worldwide church, and United Methodist Women is reaffirming its long history as a mission agency, it helps us to remember that our participation in God's mission still lies ahead of us. We can learn from the path traveled by our sisters and brothers in the past in order to be God's hands in action in today's world. J. Ann Craig graciously leads us on a thought-provoking journey full of rewarding opportunities for partnership and collaboration. She calls us to a journey of mutuality in mission.

Jorge Domingues is a former deputy general secretary with the General Board of Global Ministries.

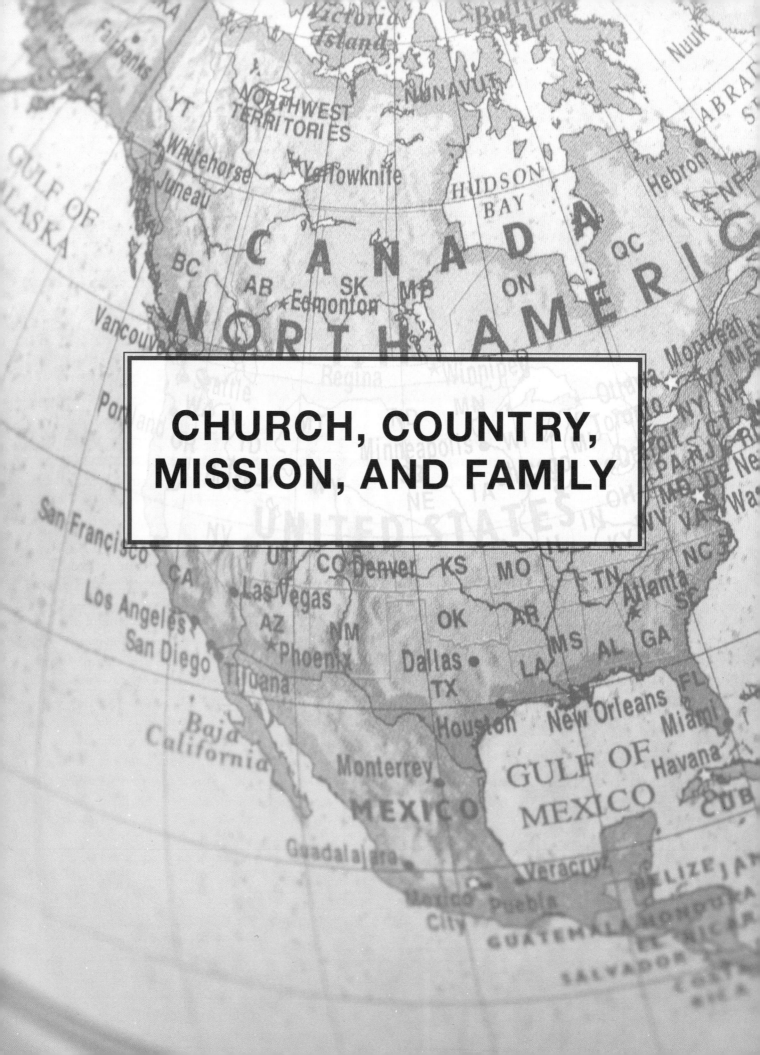

CHURCH, COUNTRY, MISSION, AND FAMILY

CHAPTER 1

This was going to be an introduction, but I thought most people would skip it to get to the "real" book. Please know that this is the real book. The first questions when you approach a book should always be: Who wrote this? Why? How does the author's story impact the content? This section provides a few insights into those questions.

The next questions should be: Who am I? Where do I come from? What impact does my life story have on how I read this content? Your own social location as a reader will shape how you understand this book: Am I like the writer? Am I like the people in the missionary conferences? Does my family come from the dominant culture, or has my family struggled to find community within the dominant culture of The United Methodist Church?

Having a sense of the author's social location and an awareness of your own is important as you walk through the geography of various people groups and churches.

Each of us has been given gifts and challenges. Sometimes our gifts come from our challenges. Whole conferences have faced their own challenges. Some have weakened or simply found new paths, while others have grown stronger and more resolute.

As I began my journey of writing about missionary conferences in The United Methodist Church, I worried that the task might be a little dry and uninteresting, but as I got more involved in the project, I realized how these missionary conferences reflect the character of The United Methodist Church, the United States, and my own story.

Both sides of my family moved through Appalachian territory, spread out across Missouri, Arkansas, and Oklahoma, and made their livings in farming, lumber, oil, politics, and the ministry. All of them were impacted by the economics and politics of slavery and the westward conquest of First Nation lands. Although my family experienced many survival challenges, as people of English, Scottish, and German heritage we benefitted from government policies. We were not among the whites who got left behind in the coal mines, enduring the exploitation of Appalachia. We kept moving west.

As people of Methodist heritage, we also reached out with the total church to help those most negatively impacted by these same policies. The past—yours and mine, individually and collectively—is as complex as our current realities. Both past and present deserve our careful attention as we continue to fulfill the Great Commandment—to love God and our neighbors as ourselves.

A Brief History

When I began this work on the missionary conferences, I picked up a book by F. M. Moore, *A Brief History of the Missionary Work in the Indian Territory: Of the Indian Mission Conference, Methodist Episcopal Church South*. The copyright is dated 1899. I was intrigued when I learned that it was the Methodist Episcopal Church (MEC) South that started the work that eventually became the Oklahoma Indian Missionary Conference.

When the Rev. Moore wrote this "brief history," so much water had already gone under the bridge, but the history of this mission work still needed to be recorded. Like many projects in the church and in our lives, such history was not easy to come by. Time passed and much of the story was inevitably lost along the way.

Moore's preface to the book is a reminder of how fleeting time is:

> The Indian Mission Conference at its session of 1892, by specific action expresses desire to have a history of its work written. . . . if any necessity ever existed for such a work, it still exists, while the facts of our earlier history are getting farther away and fewer in number as the early actors pass away, and there is not likelihood of finding literary remains among a people who could neither speak or write the English language. [1]

Seven years had passed since the first resolution to write a history of the mission work among and with native peoples was ratified. Inevitably, history was lost—but that is the nature of recording history.

You are currently reading a text on the missionary conferences written in 2015–16, thus, more than a century of activity and history has taken place since the original mission work emerged. So much of the story has been lost, and so little can be covered in one book, but my hope is that this "brief history" of our missionary conferences and study of their geography will inform our common future.

Let the Past Inform the Present

At the 2012 and 2016 General Conferences of The United Methodist Church, delegates repented for the harm done to Native Americans during the Trail of Tears, the Sand Creek Massacre, and so many other occasions, but the harm is not a thing of the past. Harm against Native Americans is ongoing. An apology is not the door to escape, but it is an opportunity to transform ourselves and the world by following the teachings of Jesus.

Moore's late-nineteenth-century reflection on Indian peoples reveals both insights and prejudices. He noted that before the Europeans arrived, there were about twenty nations and more than seven hundred languages and dialects. Yet, he could not see beyond his own culture of written literature and said there was no sign of "civilization" then or in the past. He concluded that most Native Americans are "rude, savage, and warlike people." [2]

Like so many writers about native people in that time, Moore describes them as godless:

> They had no gods, visible or invisible. There was nothing about them that would convey the idea that they had any forms of worship or that they recognized any sense of obligation as due from them to any sort of Supreme Being. The only exception to this general remark is the fact that there seemed to exist among them a belief in the "Great Spirit." But this idea wherever it existed was crude and undeveloped. [3]

In hearing what missionaries and church leaders did and said one hundred years ago, we would do well not to judge them by current norms. At the same time, we must not relegate the plain errors of understanding and outright bigotry to the past without exploring how the past informs our own ideas today. Those ideas shaped the institutions and laws that our ancestors put in place and continue to define who we are now. Few people are concerned that native peoples across this land still face gross disrespect, exclusion, and exploitation. The church is willing to apologize for a massacre one hundred years ago, but enthusiasm wanes when creating programs to address the entrenched injustices faced by First Nation people every day.

Our church was shaped by ideas about race and class that were birthed at the same time as Manifest Destiny, an ideology that promoted the westward movement of Euro Americans and a belief that Christians were destined to dominate what we now know as the United States.

Personal Connections

As I learned about the history of missionary conferences, I also learned how connected my family story is to the three conferences that we will explore in this text.

My biography is entwined with the missionary conferences.

Both sides of my family participated in the Oklahoma land grab, and my ancestors hail from the Ozark Mountains, a region deeply connected to Appalachia. When my brother moved to Alaska in the 1970s, I began to learn about the northern reaches of Methodism. Finally, I had the opportunity as National Division program staff in the 1980s to serve as the liaison to all of the mission projects in Alaska.

Of course, we have family pride in our ancestors' determination to survive, but that survival came at a high cost. By the time I was born in Oklahoma, history had set in place a world where I would encounter almost no Native Americans, despite the fact that tribes from all over this continent had been consolidated and forced to live on land in that state.

At the same time, it has been largely through The United Methodist Church that I have had the opportunity to meet Native Americans, and I am so grateful for that. Whether Houma Indians living on the bayou in Dulac, Louisiana; Eskimos in Nome, Alaska; the Navajo people in the Four Corners region; or Cherokee serving on the national board of directors of United Methodist Women, I would probably know very few people of native descent without the church.

I am grateful for the church. It is not perfect, and our members are certainly not perfect. We can be accused of working hand-in-glove with government and military forces in the mission venture, but often we have been trying to stem the tide of exploitation, harm, and death imposed on entire classes and races by military, governmental, or industrialist power brokers. As for the power brokers, they tend to tell themselves, "We are protecting our way of life." Or, "If I don't make a profit here, someone else will."

Through it all, whether in Oklahoma, Arkansas, Missouri, Nebraska, or Alaska, the church offered a social cover to my ancestors and to me. Whether it was the debilitating harm we endured as Scot-Irish highlanders, or the harm we perpetuated as invaders and land thieves, the church told us we were basically good people, loved by God. Our people strived to be good people, dedicated to God, country, and family, but the reality is much more complicated than just being a good person.

Whether in Alaska or the lower forty-eight, Native American people are still suffering the effects of invasion and cultural decimation. And indigenous people still suffer from massive unemployment, and loss of land and sea resources.

As you read this historical and geographical study on our twenty-first-century missionary conferences, think of your own biography and your family's history. Where do you come from? What harms were perpetrated on your ancestors or yourselves because of who you are or where you are from? What harms have you, your family, and your larger community inflicted on others because of who they are or where they are from?

Endnotes

1. F. M. Moore, *A Brief History of the Missionary Work in the Indian Territory: Of the Indian Mission Conference, Methodist Episcopal Church South* (Muskogee, Indian Territory: Phoenix Printing Company, 1899), preface.

2. Ibid., 6.

3. Ibid., 7–8.

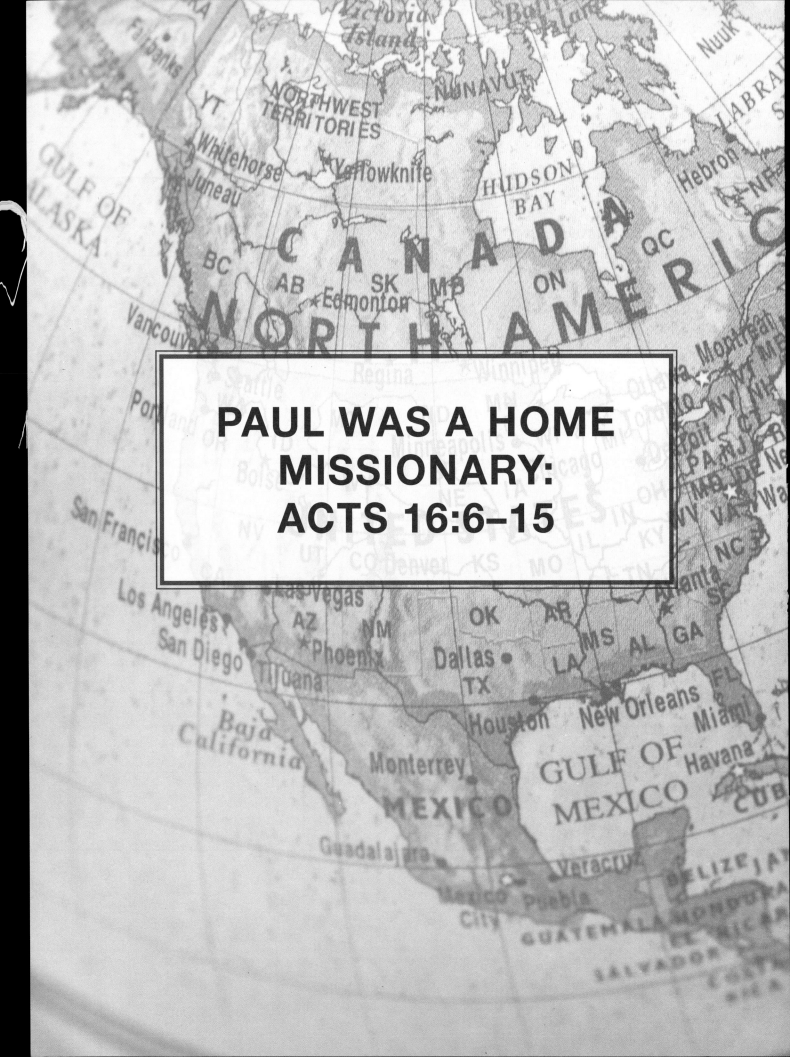

PAUL WAS A HOME
MISSIONARY:
ACTS 16:6–15

CHAPTER 2

How does the Bible inform our study of the three missionary conferences within the borders of the United States? We live in an empire context just as the early Christians lived in an empire context. The Roman Empire was the crucible for the formation of Christianity. Romans had colonized the vast region surrounding the Mediterranean Sea all the way up into what we now know as Europe.

A key difference was that Christianity emerged as a critique of religious and political oppression in the Roman Empire, but during the westward surge in North America, Christianity as the definition of "civilization" mobilized both missionary and military forces.

Paul walked the line between being a citizen of the Roman Empire and a critic of it. He was a Christian who believed the kingdom of God was much greater than any earthly kingdom or empire, but it was his membership in the earthly empire of the Romans that gave him great latitude as he moved from territory to territory.

Acts 16:6–15 provides an account of Paul and his entourage going from place to place to tell of the life, death, and resurrection of Jesus:

They went through the region of Phrygia and Galatia, having been forbidden by the Holy Spirit to speak the word in Asia. When they had come opposite Mysia, they attempted to go into Bithynia, but the Spirit of Jesus did not allow them; so, passing by Mysia, they went down to Troas. During the night Paul had a vision: there stood a man of Macedonia pleading with him and saying, "Come over to Macedonia and help us." When he had seen the vision, we immediately tried to cross over to Macedonia, being convinced that God had called us to proclaim the good news to them.

We set sail from Troas and took a straight course to Samothrace, the following day to Neapolis, and from there to Philippi, which is a leading city of the district of Macedonia and a Roman colony. We remained in this city for some days. On the sabbath day we went outside the gate by the river, where we supposed there was a place of prayer; and we sat down and spoke to the women who had gathered there. A certain woman named Lydia, a worshiper of God, was listening to us; she was from the city of Thyatira and a dealer in purple cloth. The Lord opened her heart to listen eagerly to what was said by Paul. When she and her household were baptized, she urged us, saying, "If you have judged me to be faithful to the Lord, come and stay at my home." And she prevailed upon us.

Paul was on fire for Jesus. The Holy Spirit was guiding him from place to place, culture to culture. You'll notice that the scripture above begins in the third person and then switches to a first-person point of view. Other than a few key sections, Acts is written in third person. Is this a matter of insertion? Emphasis? Biography?

"WE" went to Troas, Neapolis, and Philippi, the leading city of the Macedonia district. "WE" went outside the city gate. "WE" sat down and began to speak to the women who had gathered there.

When I studied the eras in which our three missionary conferences were founded, I was torn between thinking of these events in our church history as things that occurred long ago and things that happened almost yesterday. I felt like "We" Methodists fled starvation in Europe. "We" descended from people who traversed the Cumberland Pass near the Red Bird Mission and settled on land that belonged to Native Americans. "We" participated in the land grab in Oklahoma. "We" are the Methodists who prided ourselves in being pioneers and relied on itinerant preachers who tended to our spirits. "We" also defended the treaty rights of Cherokee and walked with them on the Trail of Tears. "We" tried to defend native peoples from the worst of military and industrial exploitation of lands and people.

"We" are complex and full of contradictions.

I wonder if Paul's travels and travel companions were so renowned that later generations wrote down the story as if they were there—as if "we" were there. Transformation happened as the gospel was preached. God walked with us and conquered death through love. "We" Christians shook the world.

We cannot stop the engagement of empires and peoples, the exchange and competition between religions, the demand for and protection of resources. It was happening in Paul's day, it set the stage for the drama of Methodism, and it is the reality for United Methodism today.

Today, we watch in deep concern as Syrian refugees flee along some of the same routes that Paul traveled. We watch from afar as people from Greece and Turkey either help or turn away refugees. We can only imagine how those who choose to help must work to navigate language, culture, and religious differences.

Mission: Challenging Social Norms

Paul's world was just as diverse, but the Roman Empire covered the entire territory of Paul's travels. His Roman citizenship gave him unearned privileges—status.[1] He was highly literate in Greek, but he also spoke to the crowd in a Hebrew dialect, probably Aramaic (Acts 22:2).

In this diverse and colonized context, Paul dreamed of a man from Macedonia urging him to "Come over to Macedonia and help us." This text is often cited when it comes to mission ventures, but it is important to note that Paul's outreach was totally within the Roman Empire. Paul was a hybrid of "home missionary" and "foreign missionary." The Roman Empire was made up of many countries and cultures, but all were dominated by one imperial power.

In this study, the three missionary conferences under discussion, the Oklahoma Indian Missionary

Conference, the Red Bird Missionary Conference, and the Alaska United Methodist Conference, are a hybrid of home and international missionary work. These conferences are a product of U.S. empire building: While some Christians were driven by the Manifest Destiny they used to rationalize grand larceny and genocide, others were inspired by the gospel to serve "the least of these" by challenging the violence of military and political domination. At the same time, they addressed the needs of those doing the invading and setting up towns in the middle of great upheaval. Most of them thought of themselves as good people.

Of course, Paul thought of himself as a good person who was following Jesus. When Paul dreamed of a man calling him to come to him, help him in Macedonia, he responded. Paul went with his entourage, but whom did they find? Women. Nothing was as they expected. On the sabbath they went to the river, where they expected to find a place of prayer. Instead, they found women by the river and spoke to them. This was where Paul met Lydia from Thyatira.

For Paul, this must have been puzzling. He was supposed to meet a man, but instead he meets a woman who is from the place near where he was staying when he had his dream. Would he have packed up and traveled with his entourage if he had a vision of a woman asking him to come to Macedonia?

Lydia was a Roman convert to the Jewish faith, a "God fearer," and she had means as a dyer of purple cloth. She and the other women from her household at the river believed and were baptized. In a spontaneous burst of generosity, she invited Paul's group to her home. They hesitated. She had to persuade them. "If you consider me a believer in the Lord," she said, "come and stay at my house." And they did, but what was at issue? Did they hesitate as men following women to their home? Was it uncomfortable for Jews to go to the home of a convert? It is not clear, but some kind of religious or cultural line was crossed. They hesitated and had to be persuaded.

As we travel together across the boundaries of missionary conferences, exploring the stories of people, churches, tribes, and conferences, there may be times when you feel uncomfortable. In those moments, think about your points of questioning or discomfort. Do not ignore them, instead explore them, and, like Lydia and Paul, know that you are traveling this path with God.

Endnotes

1. Sean A. Adams, "Paul the Roman Citizen: Roman Citizenship in the Ancient World and its Importance for Understanding Acts 22:22–29," accessed December 28, 2015, www.academia.edu/3793625/Paul_the_Roman_Citizen_Roman_Citizenship_in_the_Ancient_World_and_its_Importance_for_Understanding_Acts_22_22-29.

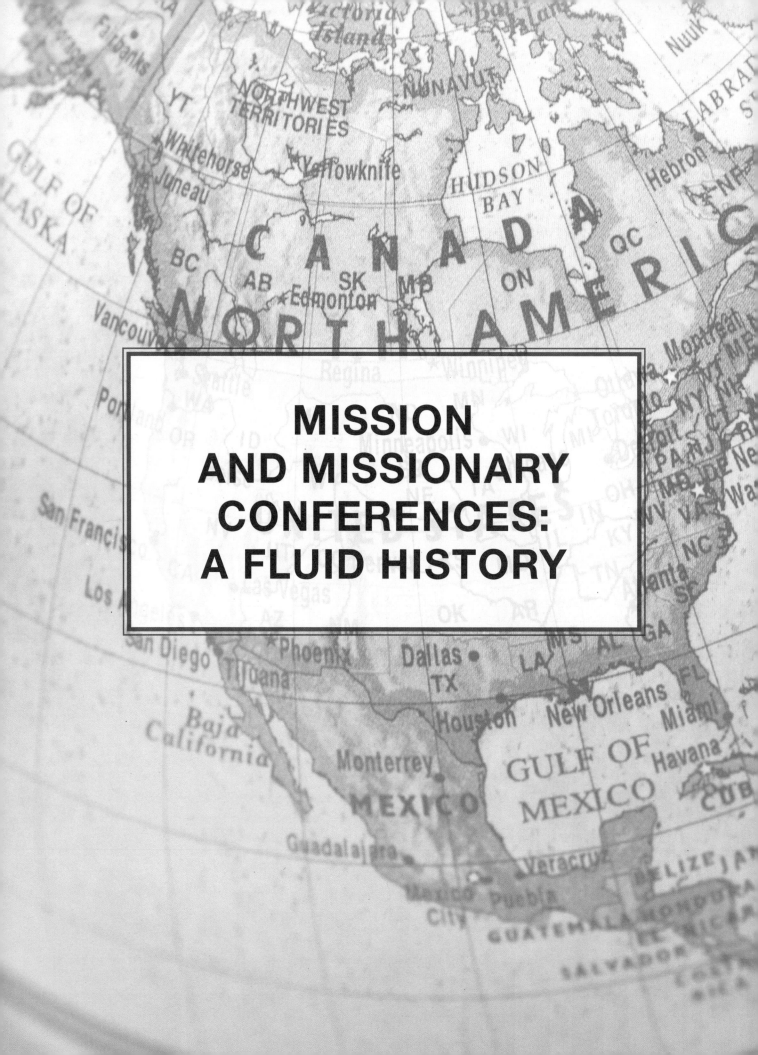

MISSION
AND MISSIONARY
CONFERENCES:
A FLUID HISTORY

CHAPTER 3

Three Missionary Conferences

Alaska United Methodist Conference

The Alaska United Methodist Conference is overseen by a superintendent who is under the administration of the Pacific Northwest Annual Conference and its bishop. The conference includes twenty-eight churches and several mission agencies that are located across the vast state of Alaska. Although "missionary" has been removed from the name of the Alaska Conference at the request of Native Americans, it still functions as a missionary conference.

Red Bird Missionary Conference

The Red Bird Missionary Conference is a small area in the mountains of the Kentucky Annual Conference that splits the Southeast District. It is about the size of the metropolitan area of Anchorage, Alaska—just for comparison. The Red Bird website lists twenty-three churches, a conference center, eight pastors and outreach workers, and four National Mission Institutions: Henderson Settlement in Frakes, Kentucky, and the Red Bird Clinic, Red Bird Mission, and Red Bird Christian School, all in Beverly, Kentucky, where the conference office is also located.

However, the history and geography of the Red Bird Missionary Conference is representative of most of the Appalachian region, which was initially populated by people seeking land and natural resources and later became isolated, impoverished, and increasingly exploited by the nation's mining and logging interests.

Oklahoma Indian Missionary Conference

The Oklahoma Indian Missionary Conference (OIMC) primarily follows the state's geographic boundaries, as does the Oklahoma Annual Conference, but there are also some OIMC congregations in Kansas and Texas. The OIMC website lists more than ninety congregations and ministries in four regions, mostly in Oklahoma.

OIMC is a vital remnant of whole nations of people that once populated the southeastern and central areas of the United States. Those in the southeast were pushed to the west by military force as a result of the Indian Removal Act. Many were Methodists and some who walked the Trail of Tears were white missionaries who fought both government and church to stand with their indigenous brothers and sisters against this injustice.

Missionary Conferences, Defined

So, with such wide-ranging geographic realities, how are the missionary conferences to be understood? *The Book of Discipline of The United Methodist Church 2016* can guide our comprehension of this matter, and all things structural in The United Methodist Church:

Section VII. The Missionary Conference

¶ 585. Definition—A conference is a missionary conference because of its particular mission opportunities, its limited membership and resources, its unique leadership requirements, its strategic regional or language considerations, and ministerial needs. The General Board of Global Ministries shall provide administrative guidance and major financial assistance, including attention to the distinctive property matters.

¶ 586. Organization—A missionary conference shall be organized in the same manner and with the same rights and powers as an annual conference (¶¶ 601–604), but with the following exceptions:

1. The College of Bishops shall provide episcopal supervision for any missionary conference(s) within its jurisdictional boundaries as are organized. The bishop thus placed in charge and having episcopal supervision within the respective episcopal area in cooperation with the General Board of Global Ministries shall appoint a conference superintendent and/or district superintendents. Such conference and/or district superintendent(s) shall be an elder(s) and shall be subject to the same limitations on years of service as district superintendents (¶ 418). Years of service may be either consecutive or non-consecutive. Years of service as a conference and/or district superintendent in a missionary conference shall be counted toward the total of twelve years permitted in a regular annual conference.[24]

2. The General Board of Global Ministries shall give close supervision and guidance in setting up the administrative and promotional budgets and Advance projects within the conference and in the promotion of new mission projects. The conference, in making requests for appropriations for support and grants and loans for building projects, shall submit to the General Board of Global Ministries a statement of the proposed annual promotional and administrative budget and the proposed financial plan for new mission and building projects. New work and building projects involving increased appropriations from the General Board of Global Ministries shall first have the approval of the General Board of Global Ministries.

3. Missionary conferences shall elect clergy and lay delegates to General and jurisdictional conference on the same basis as annual conferences as provided in ¶¶ 502 and 514.

4. a) *Membership*—A missionary conference shall determine by majority vote whether it will establish the right of full ministerial membership. With approval and consent of the bishops or other judicatory authorities involved, appointments are to be made by the resident bishop of the conference in which the clergy person is to serve.

b) An ordained minister in full connection with an annual conference who is appointed to a missionary conference that has previously voted to include full membership under § 4a may choose either to request the bishop of the missionary conference to seek the transfer of his or her membership into full membership with the missionary conference or retain his or her membership in a home conference and be considered in an affiliated relationship to the missionary conference.

c) In a missionary conference which has not voted to include full membership, each United Methodist cleric appointed by the bishop shall retain his or her membership in a home conference and be considered in an affiliated relationship to the missionary conference.

d) Affiliated relationship shall entitle the ordained minister to the fellowship of the conference, to full participation in its activities, including holding office and representing the missionary conference in General and jurisdictional conferences. An affiliate member of a missionary conference shall not vote in his or her annual conference while retaining the affiliate relationship to a missionary conference. Such affiliate relationship to a missionary conference shall be only for the duration of the ordained minister's appointment to the conference.

An affiliate member elected to a General or jurisdictional conference from a missionary conference shall not be eligible to be elected to such position from the conference where his or her membership is held.

e) A missionary conference may elect into full ministerial membership those persons desiring full membership in accordance with ¶ 588.

f) A pastor under full-time appointment in a missionary conference, upon consultation with and the approval of the bishop and conference or district superintendent or cabinet, may waive his or her claim upon the conference minimum salary. This waiver is to be reviewed annually and is to be effective until the time of subsequent appointment.

g) In a missionary conference that has not established the right of full ministerial membership (§4a), if the missionary conference is part of an episcopal area consisting of two or more annual and missionary conferences, then for purposes of candidacy for ordination (¶¶ 310–314), provisional membership (¶¶ 324–327), and election to full conference membership (¶¶ 328–336), the missionary conference may function as a district of an annual conference in the same episcopal area, with and only with the approval of the presiding bishop, the Board of Ordained Ministry of the annual conference, and the committee on ordained ministry of the missionary conference. If the missionary conference does not have a committee on ordained ministry, then approval may be provided by the body of the missionary conference to which the functions of the committee on ordained ministry have been assigned.

5. A missionary conference may include in its membership representation of such mission agencies within its boundaries as it deems advisable, provided, however, such representation shall not exceed a number equal to one-third of the total membership of the missionary conference and that such representatives shall be members of The United Methodist Church in accordance with constitutional requirements.[25]

6. In order to provide traditional and experimental ministries, the bishop of the missionary conference may appoint an effective elder to other than full-time pastoral appointment combined with secular employment. This will in no way affect the conference relationship. Pension and other benefits shall be provided in consultation with the parties involved and with the approval of the missionary conference.

7. A missionary conference that has not established the right of full ministerial membership may ordain indigenous racial and ethnic persons as deacons who, although they are not associate members, shall be accorded all the

rights and privileges of associate membership in the missionary conference, provided that they have completed all of the necessary requirements for candidacy and such other requirements the missionary conference may establish. Further, these persons have the right to pursue transfer of their ministerial relationship to another annual conference as an associate member and to pursue a relationship of full connection under the guidance of that annual conference.

24. See Judicial Council Decisions 448, 512.

25. See Judicial Council Decision 511.

¶ 587. Only the General Conference can create a missionary conference or change a missionary conference to a provisional annual conference or an annual conference. A petition to the General Conference for change in status from a missionary conference shall set forth details of the history and status of the conference and shall be accompanied by a report and recommendation of the General Board of Global Ministries.

¶ 588. *Rights and Privileges*—Missionary conferences shall have the same rights as those given to the central conferences in ¶ 543.7, .8 to make such changes and adaptations regarding the ministry and ordination of ordained ministers as the effective use of indigenous leadership in the missionary conference may require, provided that no action shall be taken that is contrary to the Constitution and the General Rules of The United Methodist Church, and provided further that a missionary conference that does not have a board of ordained ministry must use the process prescribed in ¶ 586.4.g) for approval of candidates for ordination.[1]

The Fluid Character and History of the Missionary Conferences

The opening paragraph of the preceding excerpt from *The Book of Discipline* guides us to understand a missionary conference as characterized by " . . . mission opportunities, its limited membership and resources, its unique leadership requirements, [and] its strategic regional or language considerations and ministerial needs."

The Alaska United Methodist Conference is huge, but it has been challenged by limited membership and the high cost of travel throughout the connection; it provides unique opportunities for clergy and missionaries to work in a context with many indigenous peoples and environmental concerns.

The Red Bird Missionary Conference is small with limited resources and membership, and it is located in Appalachia, where issues of poverty, economic exploitation, health, and environmental degradation from mining are all major concerns.

OIMC encompasses more congregations than the other two missionary conferences, but resources are scarce among First Nations due to a history of wars and other genocidal actions and policies, reservations, and schools designed to stop the transfer of native language and culture.

There is history of fluidity to the geographic and political boundaries that represent The United Methodist Church and its predecessor denominations. As needs arose among different language and ethnic groups, the church did constituency work and established missions that sometimes became missionary conferences, or moved directly into being conferences.

Methodism in the colonies began in population hubs such as Philadelphia and New York. In those days, all Methodist work was missionary work. In an adapted excerpt from the General Board of Global Ministries website:

> Organized Methodism in America began as a lay movement. Among its earliest leaders were Robert Strawbridge, an immigrant farmer who organized work [in] about 1760 in Maryland and Virginia, Philip Embury and his cousin, Barbara Heck, who began work in New York in 1766, and Captain Thomas Webb, whose labors were instrumental in Methodist beginnings in Philadelphia in 1767. African Americans participated actively in these groundbreaking and formational initiatives though much of that contribution was acknowledged without much biographical detail.
>
> The first conference of Methodist preachers in the colonies was held in Philadelphia in 1773 with ten lay pastors. After the Revolutionary War, Wesley sent Thomas Coke to America to superintend the work with [Francis] Asbury. In December 1784, the famous Christmas Conference of preachers was held in Baltimore at Lovely Lane Chapel to chart the future course of the movement in America. Most of the American preachers attended, probably including two African Americans, Harry Hosier and Richard Allen. It was at this gathering that the movement became organized as The Methodist Episcopal Church in America.
>
> In the years following the Christmas Conference, The Methodist Episcopal Church published its first Discipline (1785), adopted a quadrennial General Conference, the first of which was held in 1792, drafted a Constitution in 1808, refined its structure, and established a publishing house. [2]

Two major factors formed the backdrop for American Methodism, an ideology of racial, religious, and cultural superiority, paired with a belief in political, military, and colonial expansionism. The United Methodist Church and its predecessor denominations followed a parallel path in their support of the British colonization of North America. Although John Wesley, the founder of Methodism, resisted the colonists' rebellion against British rule, the success of the American Revolution made American Methodist identification with the United States rather than Britain inevitable. And both countries were propped up by the "execrable" (to use John Wesley's term) institution of slavery. [3]

Even during the formative years of the United States, slavery was contested. John Wesley condemned slavery with his whole being and expected other Methodists in America to do the same. Sadly, some white Methodists may have wanted freedom for black Americans, but they did not necessarily respect them, and it wasn't long before many African Americans broke away from the church. In 1794, after he was pulled from his knees by a white parishioner as he prayed, Richard Allen, an African-American minister, founded the African Methodist Episcopal Church in Philadelphia. In 1796, a group of African-American Methodists in New York birthed the African Methodist Episcopal Zion Church (AME Zion). In a history written in 1884, almost one hundred years after the founding of this church, and two decades after the Civil War ended, Bishop John Jamison Moore of the AME Zion Church wrote:

> When the first Methodist Episcopal Society was established in New York (whites), among whom were several colored persons, the two races found no difficulty in the reciprocity of religious fellowship, and the equal enjoyment of religious rights and privileges, but as the church grew popular and influential, the prejudice of caste began to engender negro proscription, and as the number of colored members increased, the race-friction and proscription increased, which finally overcame the tolerance of the colored members of the M. E. Society. Again the M. E. church in New York licensed a number of colored men to preach, but

prohibited them from preaching even to their own brethren, except occasionally, and never among the whites. The colored preachers, being thus deprived of the opportunity of improving their gifts and graces, as they then stood connected with the white M. E. Society, and prohibited from joining the annual M. E. conference, as itinerant preachers, with their white brethren. Thus restricted in their church relations, they were prompted to seek the privilege of holding meetings among themselves. We set forth these facts because we are frequently asked why we separated from the mother church, and why we don't now return to the mother church and let them take the supervision of us. We simply say in answer to the above query, we could not consistently return to the mother, while the radical causes exist that drove us out, which they know still exist;—race prejudice, and proscription. When we return we do not wish to be under their government, but an integral part of it. [4]

In 1845, the church divided between North and South over slavery and wouldn't be reunited until 1939 when the Northern and Southern Methodists came back together. However, the reunification agreement was made at the expense of African-American Methodists, who were relegated to a segregated Central Jurisdiction. The Central Jurisdiction was not dissolved until 1968.

In a Methodist Episcopal Church (MEC) map from 1920 (shown below), we see the politics and fluidity of conference borders, along with labels such as "missionary conference" and "ethnic work."

METHODIST EPISCOPAL CHURCH (NORTH), 1920

Detail, Boundaries of Annual Conferences, Methodist Episcopal Church, 1920.
Used by permission of the Methodist Library, Drew University.

At that time, the church was still split into MEC (North) and MEC (South), but the South was not the only place where race was a determining factor for membership. "White, English-speaking conferences" in the MEC (North) existed from coast to coast. The MEC (North) had conferences throughout the South, too, some of which extended into Mexico, without stopping at the southern border of the United States, which had been in place since the mid-1800s when the borders of Texas, New Mexico, and Arizona were well established.[5]

The small print of the MEC (North) map, at left, labeled "White, English-Speaking Conferences" says, "Excluding Norwegian and Danish work east of the Alleghenies and all French, Spanish, Portuguese, and Italian work outside of territory assigned to the Latin-American Mission."

A Denomination Shaped by Race

The United Methodist Church has always been a church shaped by race—both in our desire for fair and just relationships, as well as culturally driven forms of discrimination. John Wesley went to the Americas to convert the Indians of Georgia, but rarely came across native people. Instead, an unrequited romance with the daughter of a town official forced him to flee back to England.

Eventually, one the biggest accomplishments of his life was encouraging the English politician William Wilberforce to introduce bills in Parliament to ban the enslavement of Africans in the English Commonwealth. The last letter Wesley ever wrote was to Wilberforce, in 1791, but it was not until 1807 that the Abolition of the Slave Trade Act was signed into law, ending the slave trade in the British colonies.[6] England's stand against slavery interfaced with the growing abolitionist movement in the Americas. John Wesley and other Methodists prohibited the ownership

of slaves by Methodist clergy—until a slave was inherited by John O. Andrew, a Methodist Bishop in the South.[7] Andrew claimed innocence, since his wife had actually inherited the slave, but the event was enough to split the church in 1845, fifteen-plus years before the Civil War started.[8]

In the split, the Indian Mission Annual Conference was torn between the northern and southern branches of the Methodist Episcopal Church. It is important to note that the Indian Mission Annual Conference was not specifically a mission to Native Americans; it was new ministerial work (therefore a mission) in the Indian Territory of Oklahoma.[9] The founding of the conference in 1844 came just before the schism. Members of the Indian Mission Conference passed a resolution condemning the split but also voted to become part of the MEC (South).[10]

At the time of organization there were 27 local preachers, 85 white members, 133 Negro members and 2,992 Indian members in the Conference. During the year, $217.21 had been collected locally for missions. There were now 90,000 Indians in the Territory with some 75,000 belonging to the Five Civilized Tribes.[11]

An appendix in Homer Noley's landmark book, *First White Frost*, published in 1991, lists the presiding bishop at each annual conference of the MEC (South) Oklahoma Indian Mission.[12] Thomas Morris is well known as the first conference bishop, but what is not as well known is that Bishop James O. Andrew, the bishop whose actions precipitated the split between North and South, presided over the Indian Mission Annual Conference in both 1848 and 1853. Considering the conflict between the North and the South that instigated the split in the church, this assignment could not have been viewed as anything but another endorsement of slavery.

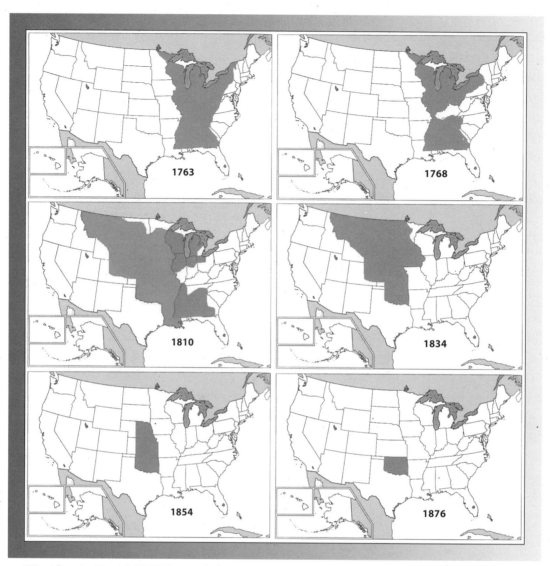

"Timeline in Maps," OK/ITGenWEb, http://www.rootsweb.ancestry.com/~itgenweb/itprojects/timeline-maps.htm.

Each year there was a census of how many whites, African Americans, and Native Americans were a part of the Oklahoma Indian Mission. While white missionaries preached to the Native Americans, only a handful of Native Americans ever preached and they were not ordained.

When the Indian Mission Conference formally became the Oklahoma Annual Conference in 1906, the organization underwent more than just a name change. White churches in what would soon become the state of Oklahoma officially laid claim to legitimacy, placing themselves alongside other conferences in the rest of the national church and pushing aside work in one of the oldest mission fields for Southern Methodism. No longer burdened with the "badge of missions," the Oklahoma Conference directed its attention toward the typical issues of buildings, money, and membership faced by other mainstream Southern Methodist conferences. [13]

As shown in the maps at left, in the Royal Proclamation of 1763, King George III designated the first official "Indian Country," which spanned from the Appalachian Mountains to the Mississippi River. After the Louisiana Purchase of 1803, "Indian Country" was pushed west of the Mississippi, opening up the eastern United States for settlement. Then, through a series of acts that forced Native Americans to cede their land and move to designated regions, "Indian Territory" was created in 1834, and then reduced until it was approximately the size of Oklahoma in 1876.

In a matter of decades, native populations were reduced from nations that spread from coast to coast to isolated reservations and small pockets of survivors. Sometimes their endurance was due to fortuitous isolation, but mostly it reflected the absolute determination of the native peoples. Churches both defended Native Americans and functioned as the instruments of their cultural decimation.

History as Told by Maps

In 1866, one year after the end of the Civil War, a map of the annual conferences of the Methodist Episcopal Church (South), shown below, reveals that their conferences followed the Mason Dixon line and included disputed territories such as Kansas and Missouri, and perhaps surprisingly, the West Coast and the Montana/Idaho region (previously known as the Missouri Territory because the headwaters of the Missouri River begin in Three Forks, Montana).

ANNUAL CONFERENCES OF
THE METHODIST EPISCOPAL CHURCH (SOUTH), 1866

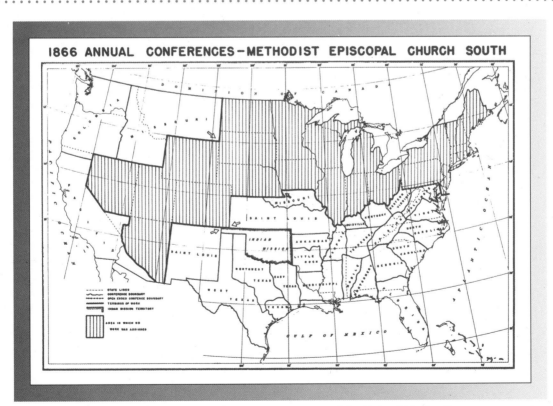

Methodist Episcopal Church (South) Map, 1866. ©1956 The United Methodist Publishing House. Used by permission. All rights reserved.

Boundaries among Methodists were created by forces that often had nothing to do with geography. For example, in a map from the 1920s, the MEC (North) delineated "White English-Speaking Conferences" with the "Colored Conferences" overlapping but separate. The South was willing to enslave people of African descent, but as this map suggests, the North seemed no more interested in worshiping with them than the Southerners. [14]

It took almost one hundred years after the schism of 1845, but in 1939, white Methodists in the North and South reunited to form the Methodist Church. Tragically and tellingly, whites brokered the reunion by institutionalizing the segregated Central Jurisdiction—institutionalizing the incipient racism of North, South, East, and West. The MEC (North) map of "Colored Conferences," shown below, graphically reveals that the sin of racism and segregation cannot be solely laid at the feet of white Southern Methodists. [15]

The reunited church was mapped in 1956, and included a white Oklahoma Conference (see map, opposite). The insert includes the Indian Mission within the same boundaries as the state of Oklahoma. Black churches in Oklahoma were included in yet another conference overlay, so Oklahoma actually had three conferences, although the black conference encompassed a wider geographic area than the others. The Indian Mission appears to have had somewhat porous boundaries as well, though the map is not very clear in this respect.

The Central Jurisdiction was disbanded in 1968 after a great struggle that included picketing of the General Conference organized by Methodist and United Brethren leaders. Leaders within the United Brethren Church (UBC) are credited with making the end of the Central Jurisdiction a requirement for joining with the Methodist Episcopal Church (MEC) to become The United

METHODIST EPISCOPAL CHURCH (NORTH), 1920

Detail, Boundaries of Annual Conferences, Methodist Episcopal Church, 1920.
Used by permission of the Methodist Library, Drew University.

ANNUAL CONFERENCES OF THE METHODIST CHURCH

Annual Conferences of the Methodist Church, 1956. ©1956 The United Methodist Publishing House. Used by permission. All rights reserved.

Methodist Church. Some of the names of the new UMC conferences, such as the Baltimore-Washington Conference, were a nod to the historically black conferences of the MEC—instead of making the white conference names the norm.

This same Methodist church map from 1956 shows the "Latin American Work" in California and Nevada, while the Rio Grande Conference covered Texas and New Mexico. The "Japanese Work" covered almost the entire country west of the Rockies.

The reason for exploring the maps of missions designated by the Methodist governing bodies is because they shape who we are as a church and a people today. Often paralleling immigration trends in the United States, some of our churches in various regions moved through periods where they spoke only German, Swedish, Japanese, Spanish, or Chinese. Some of these areas carried the title of "mission," others "conference," and others "work." The boundaries for these designations overlapped; sometimes they overlapped multiple times, as we saw in Oklahoma. They provide us with a snapshot of the conference at a particular time. They are fixed, only for the moment, but always determined by the General Conference, as is true today. For denominational merger charts that document the mergers that led to the creation of conferences in The United Methodist Church in the three regions under discussion, see Appendix A.

Language differences in the United States are still a compelling reality in mission today. There are

United Methodist churches across the United States that use some combination of English and other languages including Vietnamese, Cherokee, Tongan, Chinese, Korean, Spanish, Hmong, Creole, Samoan, Tagalog, and others. There are so many Korean congregations that, in 2004, there was an effort to create a Korean jurisdiction in the United States. It did not pass at General Conference, in part because it reminded many people of the segregated Central Jurisdiction.

What is your first language? How were your ancestors impacted by their language or ethnicity? Are there places in the United States where additional missionary conferences could function? Where and why? What would be the pros and cons?

Endnotes

1. *The Book of Discipline of The United Methodist Church 2016*, "The Missionary Conference: Definition" ¶585–88 (Nashville: United Methodist Publishing House, 2017), 388–91.

2. "Who We Are," The United Methodist Church, accessed February 17, 2016, www.umc.org/who-we-are/roots.

3. "Letter to William Wilberforce," General Board of Global Ministries, accessed June 22, 2016, www.umcmission.org/Find-Resources/John-Wesley-Sermons/The-Wesleys-and-Their-Times/Letter-to-William-Wilberforce.

4. John Jamison Moore, *History of the A.M.E. Zion Church in America: Founded in 1796, in the City of New York* (York, PA: Teachers' Journal Office, 1884), accessed February 17, 2016, http://docsouth.unc.edu/church/moorej/moore.html.

5. "The Gadsen Purchase, 1853–1854," U.S. Department of State, accessed December 5, 2015, https://history.state.gov/milestones/1830-1860/gadsden-purchase.

6. "The Letters of John Wesley: 1791," Wesley Center Online, accessed December 5, 2015, http://wesley.nnu.edu/john-wesley/the-letters-of-john-wesley/wesleys-letters-1791.

7. "The Slavery Question and Civil War (1844–1865)," UMC.org, accessed December 5, 2015, www.umc.org/who-we-are/the-slavery-question-and-civil-war.

8. Charles Elliott, *History of the Great Secession from the Methodist Episcopal Church in the Year 1845* (Swormstedt & Poe, 1855), accessed December 5, 2015, https://archive.org/details/historyofgreatse00elli.

9. Martha Stewart, "The Oklahoma Indian Missionary Conference," from *The Chronicles of Oklahoma* (Oklahoma Historical Society, 1941), 330, accessed June 22, 2016, http://digital.library.okstate.edu/Chronicles/v040/v040p330.pdf.

10. Paul D. Mitchell, *From Tepees to Towers: A History of the Methodist Church in Oklahoma* (Oklahoma Annual Conference, 1946), accessed March 6, 2016), 21, https://archive.org/stream/fromtepeestotowe01mitc/fromtepeestotowe01mitc_djvu.txt.

11. Stewart, "The Oklahoma Indian Missionary Conference," accessed December 15, 2015, http://digital.library.okstate.edu/Chronicles/v040/v040p330.pdf.

12. Homer Noley, *First White Frost: Native Americans and United Methodism* (Nashville: Abingdon Press, 1991), appendix.

13. Tash Smith, *Capture These Indians for the Lord: Indians, Methodists, and Oklahomans, 1844–1939* (University of Arizona Press, 2014), accessed August 6, 2016, page v, www.jstor.org/stable/j.ctt183p9m5.2.

14. Blake Barton Renfro, "The Reunification of American Methodism, 1916–1939," Master's Thesis, March 2010, accessed December 5, 2015, http://etd.lsu.edu/docs/available/etd-04292010-132837.

15. Detail, Boundaries of Annual Conferences, Methodist Episcopal Church, 1920. Used by permission of the Methodist Library, Drew University.

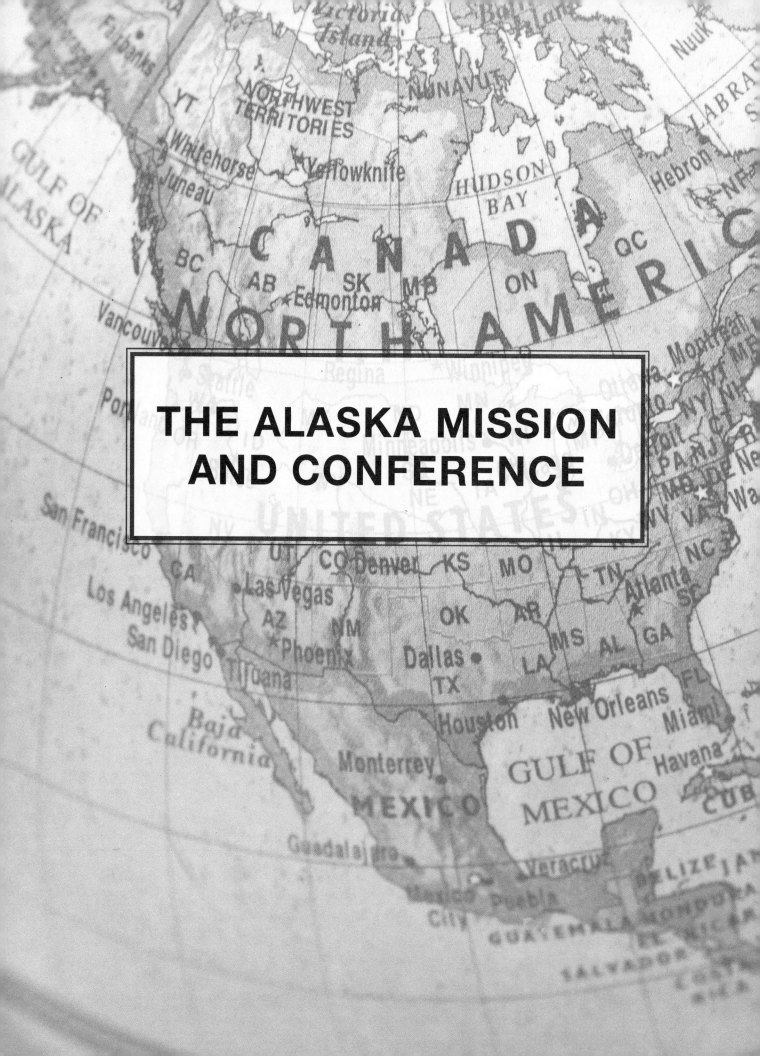

THE ALASKA MISSION AND CONFERENCE

CHAPTER 4

Ministry Beginnings

Early Methodist missionary outreach in Alaska began in 1877 along the southern coast in Wrangell, near Alaska's border with British Columbia, by the Rev. Thomas Crosby, pastor of the Fort Simpson Methodist Church.[1] One year after Dr. Sheldon Jackson was appointed general agent for education in Alaska, he sent John and Ethelda Carr to start a school and church in Unga in the Shumagin Islands, halfway out on the chain of Aleutian Islands. "The Woman's Home Missionary Society of the Methodist Episcopal Church furnished support and travel money for Mrs. Carr. Methodist work carried on sporadically in Unga until about 1953."[2]

Near the end of the century, after gold had been discovered along the Klondike River in 1896, Charles McCabe, presiding bishop of the growing Western Norwegian-Danish Conference of the Methodist Episcopal Church, began pushing for a mission in Alaska.[3] By 1897, the gold rush surged with thousands of "stampeders" thronging to find gold.[4] Some 100,000 people set out for the Klondike River, but less than half had enough fortitude, equipment, or luck to make it to the gold fields.[5] What they found was a rugged land, quite similar to the terrain in Scandinavian countries.

In dozens of letters written by Norwegians and Norwegian Americans in the late 1890s and the early 1900s the expressions "New Norway" and "New Scandinavia" appear as naturally, if not as frequently, as comments about weather, the sea, mountains, forests, and tundra.[6]

Carl J. Larsen, presiding elder of the Alaska District, traveled from Seattle to Alaska where he set up a tent along the trail to the gold fields and began to preach in October 1897.

> Finally, he left for Seattle from Unalaska on September 25, 1898, having traveled 11,290 miles, 1,670 of which were by rowboat and 150 on foot. Upon returning to California Larsen was appointed by Bishop McCabe to serve Juneau, the place which was considered the most promising for permanent work.[7]

Explorers, retailers, miners, and other preachers also headed to Alaska. A team lead by E. H. Harriman observed that:

> The Gold Rush was in full swing, salmon canneries were working round the clock, and fur seal rookeries exported thousands of skins every year. The Native cultures were contending with a growing tourist community, and subsistence practices were

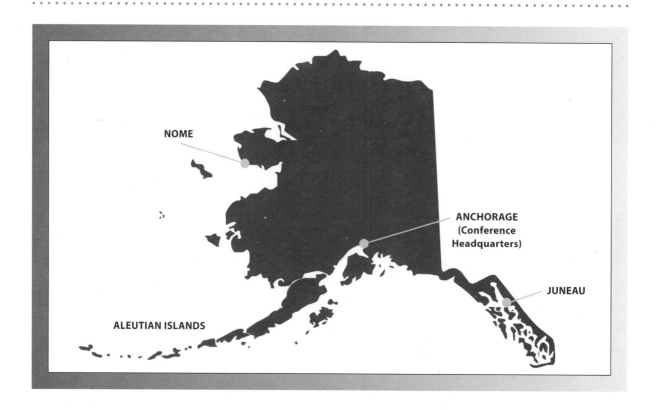

giving way to a new economy of gold, fish and fur. The Harriman scholars of 1899 observed and catalogued what they saw: a gloriously beautiful land on the cusp of inevitable and sometime devastating change. [8]

In 1904, Alaska was recognized by the General Conference as an official mission outreach, and the project begun by a bishop and a missionary became official. [9]

Alaska's history is ancient, dating back to the Paleolithic Era. Archaeological sites in the region have been explored in recent years, resulting in sometimes controversial claims about early humans traveling there by boat across the Bering Sea or migrating by foot from Siberia to Alaska across the Bering Strait, which some scientists speculate was a wide swath of land at one point. [10]

Given the curiosity, creativity, and persistence of human beings, it seems likely that they came to Alaska using various forms of transport, making their way down the coast and then inland beginning some 14,000 years ago. [11]

In the mid-1600s, Russian traders began traveling to Alaska. By the mid-1700s, Vitus Bering made it to the shores off Kayak Island and then traveled to the Shumagin Islands where he interacted with indigenous populations and recorded ethnographic information. Another Russian ship was blown off course, landing to the south, where its crew is said to have become part of the Tlingit people.

Eventually, Alaska Natives became integral to the fur trading business. How the traders treated them was of deep concern to priests of the Russian

Orthodox Church when they arrived in the region in the 1790s. The priests provided religious instruction to the native peoples and became a buffer to the harshest treatment by traders.

In 1796, the Orthodox priest Hieromonk Makarii took six Aleuts to St. Petersburg, Russia, to appeal to the Czar to stop Russian abuse of native people. The Czar met with the Aleuts but to no avail. Only one Alaska Native and the priest survived the trip home. [12]

In the Aleutian Islands, the Russians ravaged the otter and seal populations and the local economy as they forced experienced hunters to abandon their villages and families to work for them. Sometimes they held villagers hostage in exchange for more fur hunting. Between European diseases and starvation due to the theft of the Aleut's best hunters, more than half of the Aleut population had died by the mid-1880s. [13]

Sheldon Jackson and His Mission to Alaska Natives

By the time Alaska was sold by Russia to the United States in 1867, the pattern of exploitation of natural resources that left Alaska Natives bereft of adequate hunting opportunities was well established.

Methodists arrived in the late 1800s as the Russians were taking their leave. Christianity had been preached in most parts of Alaska, primarily through the Russian Orthodox tradition.

Presbyterians arrived almost simultaneously with the Methodists. Both Methodists and Presbyterians were focused on the miners seeking gold. Even missionary work was competitive. One man who was very passionate, and even aggressive, in his efforts was Sheldon Jackson, a Presbyterian missionary who was a prolific church starter and organizer.

Jackson's impact on Alaska cannot be overstated. We will see that he was highly influential on the scope and character of early Methodist missions as well. He was driven by the gospel and his own ego. He was viewed by some as a figure of salvation; by others, he was a master manipulator set on dominating Alaska as well as his own denomination. [14] Jackson was also connected to the work with native peoples in the area around the Oklahoma Indian Missionary Conference.

When the transcontinental railroad was completed in 1869, Jackson headed west. He received a free pass on the railway, so he could get on and off at will. He founded hundreds of churches by convening Presbyterians at every whistle stop and pronouncing them a church! His aggressive church planting is both lionized and disparaged. Many churches disbanded shortly after they had been founded. To avoid oversight, Jackson set up a personal account to pay for his outreach efforts, which he called the Raven Fund. [15]

He was adept at working around denominational structures and tended to make emotional appeals for money to the wives of wealthy men. [16] Because he had his own fund, he could tell the Presbyterian Board of Missions that he was working as a volunteer so they could not control him. In the meantime, he was growing his Raven Fund by siphoning off mission dollars from people who thought he was under the administration of the Presbyterian Board of Missions. Jackson was not confronted by the church because it would have created too much controversy.

Early in his career, Jackson had been turned away from international mission work since he was only five feet tall and his eyesight was poor.

Jackson traveled extensively in Alaska to preach the gospel. His fortitude and dedication were nothing short of mythic. His arrival just before the Methodists was an intentional effort to stake out a claim for the Presbyterians.

> [M]y going to Alaska when I did, prevented the Methodists from occupying the ground . . . the impression had somehow been given and the expectation created that the Methodists would occupy the place. . . . If [Amanda McFarland] had not gone up at that time to remain, the Methodists would have been on the field, and perhaps the Roman Catholics. [17] [Amanda McFarland founded a major school for native girls.]

Before long, Jackson had made strong political ties to government officials. By 1885, Jackson was appointed the U.S. general agent for education in Alaska and proceeded to divide up the Alaska territory, assigning various denominations to specific regions—just as had been done among Native Americans in the West. In 1819, the U.S. government set aside $10,000 to pay missionaries and others of "good moral character" to "civilize" whole cultures through forcing children into schools, banning the use of native languages, and denigrating native religious practices. [18] This policy of assimilation meant that the government and churches were working hand in hand. There was little, if any, separation of church and state. [19]

Other historians think of Jackson as a reformer and a preserver of Alaska Native villages and families.

> In 1885 Dr. Sheldon Jackson, Presbyterian missionary to Alaska and former superintendent of the Rocky Mountain district of the Presbyterian Board of Home Missions, was appointed by the U.S. Secretary of the Interior to be General Agent of Education in Alaska, serving under the immediate supervision and jurisdiction of the U.S. Commissioner of Education. Jackson's responsibility was to make provisions for the education of children in Alaska towns and villages "without regard to race." Under his tutelage, schools were established in most native villages, and separate schools for white and native children in Alaska's few "white" towns. Jackson remained general agent until 1907, and early education in Alaska clearly carried the stamp of his dynamic personality and educational philosophy. [20]

Jackson's work in Alaska was informed by his first missionary assignment to the Choctaw Indians near the border of Arkansas and Oklahoma. His later assignments were to tribes and reservations further west, where tribes were assigned to specific denominations. By the time Alaska came into focus for Protestant missionaries, the government policy of assimilation through schools had become the norm.

> Not surprisingly, the timing of Jackson's endeavors coincided with the efforts of the Bureau of Indian Affairs and the missionary reformers to civilize the native population. Their idea of civilizing the Indians was acculturation which meant replacing their culture with the white man's culture. It also meant that the Indians could no longer speak their own languages. They must only speak English. To implement this policy, Jackson instructed his missionary teachers, and the natives who attended the schools, to speak only English. . . .
>
> The Indian reform groups believed that assimilation was the only viable alternative to extermination of the native population. Jackson's work was an extension of their philosophy and he embraced it with open arms. He and the reform groups were confident that through education, they could wipe out thousands of years of traditions and culture and turn the Indians into white men in one generation. They mistakenly believed that if one generation was exposed to American values, they would teach those who came after them. [21]

Larry Hayden, historian for the Alaska United Methodist Conference, describes how Jackson brought Methodists and other denominational leaders together so they would do their work cooperatively, rather than competitively, through a "comity" agreement:

Since there were not enough Presbyterian pastors/educators to cover such a large land area, Jackson decided to call a meeting with representatives of other interested denominations to seek their support. This happened in January 1890 at the Methodist Book Rooms in New York, where he revealed his outline for Alaska.

At this session, several churches agreed to take on mission work in different areas of the vast territory. Baptists would begin in Kodiak and the Cook Inlet area; Episcopalians would continue work already begun by Canadian Anglicans along the Yukon River, and also help along the Arctic Coast; the Methodists planned to begin mission work in the Aleutian Islands, the Moravians would start in the Kuskokwim region, the Congregationalists, the Cape Prince of Wales area, and Presbyterians would continue in [the] Southeast and along the northern Arctic Coast. Exposing a long-standing prejudice against Catholics, Jackson excluded them from the initial apportionment. Nevertheless, Catholic missions took hold on the lower Yukon. The Quakers arrived in 1895. [22]

In a 1908 homage to the mission work of Jackson, Robert Laird Steward, D.D., described the scene at this meeting where the division of territory took place:

And now I see these four heads bending over the little table, on which Sheldon Jackson has spread out a map of Alaska. For the first time they see its tremendous proportions, as it reaches over many degrees of longitude and far up into the Arctic circle [sic]. The allotment was made in perfect harmony.

As the Presbyterians had been the first to enter Southeastern Alaska, all agreed that they should retain it, untroubled by any intrusion. By the same rule, the Episcopalians were to keep the valley of the Yukon, where the Church of England, following in the track of the Hudson Bay Company, had planted its missions forty years before. The island of Kadiak [sic], with the adjoining region of Cook's Inlet, made a generous portion for the Baptist brethren; while to the Methodists were assigned the Aleutian and Shumagin Islands. The Moravians were to pitch their tents in the interior —in the valleys of the Kusko Kwim and the Nushkagak; while the Congregationalists mounted higher to the Cape Prince of Wales, on the American side of the Bering Strait; and, last of all, as nobody else would take it, the Presbyterians went to Point Barrow, in latitude seventy-two degrees and twenty-three minutes, the most northern mission station in the world.

Thus, in the military assignment of posts to be held, the stout-hearted Presbyterians at once led the advance, and brought up the rear in a climate where the thermometer was at times sixty-five to seventy degrees below zero—a situation that called for no ordinary amount of "grit and grace." [23]

Yes, there were ego-driven missionaries whose modus operandi was to manipulate or bypass church structures. But even in Jackson's case, he tried to work cooperatively and created programs that The United Methodist Church would probably fund if they were conceived today. To supplement the dwindling fishing and hunting along the coast, he mobilized the importation of small herds of domesticated caribou (reindeer) from Lapland. Jackson was able to work his government connections to get funding to import the reindeer, along with experienced herders to train Alaska Natives to tend them. It was a tenuous venture, but from those herds, the population grew to 650,000.

Predictably, as the herds became economically viable, a few white owners began to take over the industry. An Alaskan law had to be passed to force whites to sell their reindeer to the government, who moved them back into the hands of Alaska Natives.[24] Reindeer still populate Alaska and are part of the political, natural, and arguably religious landscape of the state. Efforts continue to make reindeer part of the overall economy of Alaska.[25]

The Nome Community Center

Reindeer herding was the first major program established in Nome, in the Bering Strait region, by the Woman's Home Missionary Society of the Methodist Church in 1910, fifteen years after Jackson first began organizing his reindeer-herding project. The Nome Community Center's website reads:

> Nome Community Center traces its roots to a reindeer-herding project begun in 1906. Mrs. R.H. Young, Bureau Secretary of Alaska, supplied a generous donation to the Woman's Home Missionary Society of the Methodist Church to establish a reindeer mission at Sinuk River. The purpose of the mission was to preserve and protect the tradition of reindeer herding. The mission was named the Lavina Wallace Young Mission in honor of its personal benefactor.
>
> In 1911 the reindeer-herding project extended from the Sinuk River to Sandspit, a beachfront area of Nome. Two years later, the Young Mission leased space in the Methodist Church building and opened its doors to the public. Church services, clubs, choirs, classes, workshops, Sunday school, the Epworth League [a Methodist young adult association], and recreation programs were among the services provided.[26]

Eventually, the Lavina Wallace Young Mission was housed in a separate building from the church. In response to the Civil Rights movements of the 1960s, home missions began to emphasize empowerment rather than dependence, so in 1970, it became the Nome Community Center, an independent nonprofit 501(c)(3) organization. With local control and nonprofit standing, the Nome Community Center was able to access funding sources through foundations and the government that were not available to church-operated organizations.

The Nome Community Center was an independent agency, but like most agencies founded by the women's mission programs of the church, ownership of the facility was maintained by United Methodist Women through the "Agreements of 1964" when General Conference imposed an organizational structure for the Woman's Division. These agreements were hard-won by the women of the church, since the assets and funds of the women became a target in the time period leading up to the merger of the Evangelical United Brethren (EUB) and the Methodist Church.

The building was available rent free, as long as the Nome Community Center staff and board implemented programs in keeping with the mission of United Methodist Women and United Methodist Women covered major maintenance and insurance costs. All mission agencies, and properties owned by United Methodist Women, remain linked to The United Methodist Church through a covenant agreement with United Methodist Women, and Nome Community Center remains a UMW National Mission Institution today.

In Nome, besides the community center and the church, the mission program included Maynard-McDougall Memorial Hospital. The hospital in Nome was turned over to the native corporation of that area not long after the Alaskan Native Claims Settlement Act was signed into law by President Richard Nixon in 1971.

These native corporations were established through this 1971 act in order to prevent Alaskan Native lands from disappearing into private or corporate ownership, by individuals or oil companies. The corporations were allotted 40 million acres of land for division among twelve regional native corporations and 220 village corporations. Using the business model of corporations, the native corporations became both the holding companies and regional governing bodies of this land and were not permitted to sell it for twenty years.[27]

Today, the Nome Community Center main offices are on the second floor of the Nome United Methodist Church. The community center functions under the auspices of the Boys and Girls Club of Nome and the XYZ Senior Center, a part of the community center's work that has been relocated to Division Street, where it provides seniors' meals and other services.

Methodists have had a unique ministry with Alaska Natives in Nome since the beginning. The first church in Nome was Congregational and was partly funded by the gold miners. Once gold fever faded and most of the gold mining equipment was abandoned and became part of the landscape, the churches consolidated to create a white church and a separate native church. The Methodists led the native church. At the time, the Methodists also ran a home for children and still owned the small hospital in Nome.[28]

These programs were begun by the Woman's Home Missionary Society, staffed by deaconesses, and were supported by the Woman's Division (now United Methodist Women) when Alaska became a missionary conference.

The Nome Community Center and another program, the Jesse Lee Home for Children, are the most well known of the Methodist mission projects in Alaska.

The Jesse Lee Home

The Jesse Lee Home became Alaska Children's Services and is now called AK Child & Family. The original Jesse Lee Home was established in 1890 in Unalaska, where it provided a home for hundreds of children before it moved to Seward in 1925. With larger and more accessible facilities that also included an infirmary, the mission could better serve the wider Alaskan community. Although the home moved to Anchorage after the 1964 earthquake, the clinic stayed in Seward and eventually became a nursing home. It is now the Wesley Rehabilitation and Care Center.

Interestingly, Sheldon Jackson also had a hand in the founding of the Jesse Lee Home.

Jackson was the territorial director of education in Alaska, and assigned Agnes Soule, a territorial teacher, to go to Unalaska in the Aleutian Islands chain.[29] She began to take children into her own home for education and it became apparent that some of the children also needed housing.

Soule's father was a Methodist bishop, so Jackson encouraged her to contact him about the situation and, together, they began to move the gears of decision making; in 1890, the Methodist women in mission provided the funds for a home for orphans with two buildings.[30] According to the AK Child & Family website, in Unalaska alone, Soule served hundreds of children and along the way, married Dr. Albert Newhall, who directed the home until it was transferred to Seward. Together they housed, taught, and provided medical care for the children.[31]

During World War I, a flu epidemic was ravaging the lower forty-eight states. The epidemic had not reached the children of the orphanage and missionaries in the Aleutian Islands, but it was only a matter of time. In 1919, influenza arrived in the islands; the following is one account from

Family After All: Alaska's Jesse Lee Home, Vol. I, Unalaska, 1889–1925 by Raymond L. Hudson:

The winter was stormy, but the general health of the people at Unalaska remained good. By spring, the threat seemed to have passed and life returned to normal. Dr. Newhall made a slightly ironic list of things to be thankful for: the local boys who had served in the war were unharmed; the flu had spared the village; snow was only five feet deep between the two Jesse Lee Home buildings; it was too stormy to dig clams, but plenty of clams were still waiting on the beach; the store was out of white sugar and table salt, but soft coal was only $25 a ton. [32]

When the flu hit, it was devastating.

On Wednesday morning, May 28, the Unalga tied up at the A.C. Co. dock in order to be better able to deliver assistance. Five people had died since the illness began. Dodge [the Coast Guard captain] inspected the village, the Dutch Harbor settlement, and the naval radio station near Dutch Harbor. The magnitude of what he found was reflected in the repetition of his report:

". . . native population all down and helpless, unable to cook or care for themselves in any way. All teachers and inmates of the Jesse Lee Home sick and helpless, all government school teachers sick and helpless, the people at the jail and A.C. Company house sick and helpless, all at U.S. Naval Radio Station sick and helpless, except the Chief Operator who is working night and day. . . ."

Dr. Newhall was one of the first to fall ill. He was bedridden, and within a short time the entire staff followed. Only five children escaped. Simeon Oliver remembered that Benny Benson was one of these. "Why he didn't come down with it, no one seemed to know," Simeon said, "probably too ornery or something of this sort. He was a lonely boy. We'd hear him outside singing to himself. He never strayed far from our open windows. We could always hear him singing or talking to himself or tapping stones. There wasn't even a dog around with which he could play." [33]

The flu epidemic had wiped out whole villages along the Aleutians. Six years later, in 1925, the Newhall's worked with Methodist women to move the Jesse Lee Home to Seward, then the largest port in Alaska, and built a better orphanage. [34]

More than thirty years before Alaska became a state, the Alaska Department of the American Legion sponsored a contest for Alaskan children to design the Alaska Territory flag. Benny Benson, the lonely boy who sang to himself and survived the epidemic, competed against 142 other children—but his design won. An orphan living at the Jesse Lee Home designed the Alaska state flag. [35]

The Jesse Lee Home was in Seward from 1925 through the Good Friday Earthquake in 1964. In the early 1950s, Gene Brown lived for several years in the orphanage in Seward with his parents. His firsthand account captures some of the culture shock experienced by children from Alaska Native communities:

[Jesse Lee Home] occupied many acres, including a headmaster's house that sat facing the mountains, three large buildings, aligned in a straight row perpendicular to the mountains and connected by long hallways, several farm buildings, sheds, and a barn. The Home was as self-sufficient as possible, with a large vegetable garden and the normal edible farm animals—pigs, chicken, beef—that were for the Home's use as well as for sale in Seward.

Most of the children at the Home were orphans. They came from all around Alaska; their hometowns were the fishing villages in Southeastern Alaska, or Eskimo villages on the slopes of the

Brooks Range, or the Aleut villages along the Aleutian Islands. Who can now remember them all? But the children, while having a materially better life at the Home than they could have ever had alone in the world, were social misfits in Seward, and many of the older boys, in particular, could not bear to grow up away from their clans, their families, and their customs.

Many of them ran away.

I remember one Sunday after we had all returned to the Home in the rickety old yellow buses with "Jesse Lee Children's Home" painted in black on the sides and back door, one of the Aleut "A" boys, was reported missing from his table at lunch.

Customarily we would go directly from the buses to our dorms, leave our Sunday School papers on our beds, wash our hands and line up for the walk down the long hallway to the dining hall. We each had an assigned seat: The boys sat on the side of the room nearest their hallway and the girls on the other. The service area was in the center, and that is where the staff tables were set up. They could easily see the whole dining area and take corrective action whenever one of their charges committed a breach of table etiquette.

This "A" boy didn't go to the dorm, and wasn't at his seat at lunch. After a quick search of the buildings, the male members of the staff—my father, Mr. McKinley, some of the other adult men, and several of the other "A" boys, plus my two older brothers—armed themselves with rifles, and set out to track him down. The rifles, we were always told, were in case the group encountered any black bear or moose along the way.

There was only one way off the peninsula: Follow the highway and railroad tracks through the mountain passes towards Anchorage. Many of the boys who ran away tried to hitch rides along the

highway, and some were successful. Others would lie in wait alongside the tracks for a slow moving freight train to pass by. They would then jump aboard and head for freedom.

After the men left, none of us younger children could finish eating, we were so excited. Despite the frequency of its occurrence, a runaway was still cause for great excitement and consternation at the Home: excitement amongst the children and consternation amongst the house parents.

Later that evening the men returned with the "A" boy, handcuffed and walking with his head down, held firmly by two of them.

I do not know what happened to him, or to any of the others who ran away. I only know that they felt they were imprisoned at Jesse Lee Home, and their talk was constantly of their escape and eventual return to their own people.

I hope they all made it. [36]

During World War II, the home was evacuated and Fort Raymond was established on the property. The buildings were painted in camouflage as protection from possible air strikes. Sadly, in the islands from whence Benny and many of the children had come, the Unangan/Aleuts [37] were not trusted by the U.S. military.

The history of violence, disrespect, and genocide against native peoples by the United States is long and deep. Churches have both facilitated and ameliorated its effects.

When the Jesse Lee Home was occupied by the U.S. military, the children were removed and most educational activities were interrupted. Eventually, World War II passed, and Alaska regained its footing. The school resumed serving children until a day when the earth shook.

SPOTLIGHT ON HISTORY

The Aleutian Islands, the birthplace of so many of the Jesse Lee residents, were targeted by Japan during World War II. U.S. authorities evacuated 881 Unangan people from nine villages as a response to the Japanese aggression. Most of them were allowed only one suitcase and were moved on cramped ships as they watched their homes and churches burn to make the area useless to potential Japanese invaders.[38]

The Unangan people were moved to what were known as "duration villages" in Southeast Alaska. These "villages" were makeshift camps in former canneries, a herring saltery, and a gold mine camp with dilapidated facilities and without sufficient infrastructure. They survived on tainted water and low-quality food and lived without proper homes, or warm clothes, making it a struggle to survive the two years they were interned there. "Illness of one form or another struck all the evacuees, but medical care was often nonexistent, and the authorities were dismissive of their complaints. . . . Thirty-two died at the Funter Bay camp, seventeen at Killisnoo, twenty at Ward Lake, five at Burnett Inlet. With the death of the elders so, too, passed their knowledge of traditional Unangax ways."[39]

Being resourceful, the Unangan people made the best of their situation by building and repairing their camps. They also created a makeshift church and brought their religious articles with them.[40]

As Margaret Snider, the author of *Joined and Held Together: A Children's Study on Missionary Conferences,* points out, "This forced removal of the Unangan people from their homes on the Aleutian Islands echoed the genocidal racism, violence, and destruction that are part of the history of the United States' relationships with native people groups."[41]

All of Alaska lost its sense of security as a result of the earthquake on Good Friday, March 27, 1964. Seward, where the Jesse Lee Home was then located, was devastated. The home escaped total destruction, but the children had to be evacuated.

Assessing the situation, United Methodist Women (Woman's Division of the Board of Missions) decided the cost of repairing the structures was prohibitive, and since Seward had fewer services than Anchorage, the Jesse Lee Home was moved to Anchorage. The women bought twenty-five acres of land in south Anchorage and built four residential cottages, an administrative building, and housing for the director. Later, the Benny Benson Recreation Center was added to the campus.[42]

AK Child & Family

Children returned to the Jesse Lee Home, now located in Anchorage, in January 1966. As in orphanages across the country, foster care, social services, and mental health services began to emerge. The Jesse Lee Home merged with the Lutheran Youth Center and the Anchorage Christian Children's Home in 1970. The resulting organization was named Alaska

Children's Services and became a joint mission of The United Methodist Church, the Evangelical Lutheran Church in America, and American Baptist Churches, USA.

Alaska Children's Services provided group homes, mental health services, emergency shelter, case management, and adventure-based programs to assist children and teens, including those with severe emotional and behavioral problems. Eventually, seven residential cottages on two campuses, including the original Jesse Lee Campus, was the basis for accreditation by the Joint Commission on Health Care Organizations in 1990, and they have maintained accreditation ever since.

With its strong denominational connections, Alaska Children's Services offered a spiritual life program that more than three-quarters of residential students choose to attend.

As the desire to keep families together grew in the 1990s, Alaska Children's Services began providing home-based care that included individual and group therapy, skill development, activity therapy, and case management, as well as foster-care treatment.

In 2013, the organization was renamed AK Child & Family to remove confusion between this mission and the state Office of Children's Services and to carry on the tradition of care started at the Jesse Lee Home, " . . . one child, one family at a time." [43]

AK Child & Family is a great example of a successful partnership between faith groups and the government. The land, which was originally the Jesse Lee Home property, is owned by United Methodist Women. For many years, the home has worked with the State of Alaska and relevant foundations to fully fund the multimillion-dollar annual budget to serve Alaska's children. Three denominations have come together to share properties and resources, to apply for government grants to serve children, and to create an environment where spiritual resources are provided, but participation is not required or coerced.

The Relationship between Church and State

Church organizations have seen a wide range of relationships between church and state. In Sheldon Jackson's day, it was normal for the government to give church people and groups assignments and funding with no restrictions about evangelizing and proselytizing using government money.

In the 1970s, many church-sponsored social service groups became 501(c)(3) not-for-profits and distanced themselves from their church roots to make their groups more likely to receive government and foundation grants. Property ownership and liability issues brought many church agencies in the United Methodist network back to their parent agency for accountability in the 1980s. Since then, United Methodist home missions have had a covenant agreement that specifies programs that reflect shared values and requires fiscal best practices and accountability.

In the days of Jackson and the founding years of Methodist and our predecessor denominations, melding church and state interests was expected. We might worry that Sheldon Jackson was tasked by the government to divide Alaska Natives into geographic units and assign those units to denominations, and that schools were and continue to be a strategy to "civilize" indigenous people so that they would start acting like people of the dominant culture, but suffice it to say, we are still finding our way, seeking best practices that preserve ancient cultures while equipping people to live in multiple worlds.

Continued on page 40

IN CONVERSATION

Thom White Wolf Fassett shares his thoughts on mission work in Alaska.[44]

Presbyterian, Episcopalian, Methodist were the primary denominations that established work. Because Alaska was the last frontier it sometimes attracted "loose cannon" types of people.

Methodist women did a good job in Alaska. They were there first to help set up an orphanage in Unalaska. Peter Gordon Gould grew up in the orphanage and eventually headed a section of the Board of Missions and oversaw the mission in Alaska. He also founded Alaska Methodist University.

From the beginning, Methodists focused mostly on serving Anglos, but they supported the ministry in Nome as their outreach to indigenous people. In Nome it was a combination of United Methodist and Presbyterian ministries. . . .

My first trip to Alaska was in 1978, when I was asked to work with the Eskimo whaling commission to work out the problems around the banning of all whaling by the International Whaling Commission. Before it was over, the Eskimos won and they were allowed limited kills per year. It was the big whaling operations from Russia and the USA that had almost wiped out the whale population, not the Alaska Natives.

In 1983, Bishop Cal McConnell recruited me to be the district superintendent for Alaska. When I was there, the native peoples in the UMC found out that an outsider from the UMC was there who challenged the seeming lack of interest of the Alaska Missionary Conference in the native populations.

While I was in Alaska, I worked to change that. I tried to get the church involved in the efforts to establish land rights for Alaska Natives through the Alaska Native Claims Settlement Act. Native populations were very concerned they were going to lose their land. Through the act, they were able to retain their land, but the law required that the land be divided among members. That meant the land was taxable and could eventually be sold. The native corporations were established, but consultants ripped them off and the church seemed unwilling or unable to advocate for justice in the situation.

Although this act was signed at Alaska Methodist University (changed to Alaska Pacific University in the 1980s), indigenous people were not a priority of the conference. Local churches and the conference faced the high prices in Alaska and focused more on setting up churches for oil immigrants and keeping their membership numbers up than on ministries to indigenous peoples. . . .

. . . moving clergy and expanding ministry with Alaska Natives cost money. We were able to raise money from the lower forty-eight through some innovative sales of souvenirs, such as hats from the whaling commission with the designs of native artist Caleb Wengary.

We were able to initiate new ministries in Nome and Anchorage with the leadership of Walter Moffett in the urban setting. Few Alaska Natives were in leadership among United Methodist Alaskans, but while I was there, we called Della Waghiyi as an indigenous lay pastor, and she was eventually the first Alaska Native person ordained in The United Methodist Church. . . .

It is important to note that Alaska never signed any treaties with the federal government. There were no wars—just a steady takeover of lands and culture. Fortunately, efforts emerged in the 1970s to stem that tide. Native cultural practices were encouraged in and out of church settings and government officials recognized they could avoid some of the devastating mistakes made in the lower forty-eight.

Watching from a distance today, it looks like Alaska is facing many of the challenges every conference faces—lower membership and rising costs. Some churches have closed, but there is still work that could emerge. Presbyterian and Episcopalian churches have more Alaska Natives in leadership and we could do more. Like everywhere, fundamentalist ideas are spreading, but Methodists have a more open theology that people need to know about.

But the denomination needs to step up and support native leaders in Alaska and places like the Oklahoma Indian Missionary Conference, where the salaries are far lower than in the rest of the church. Youth are leaving the church because they see the disparities. There are few national staff and little work among native peoples. We can do better.

Like many conferences, the Alaska United Methodist Conference struggles with maintaining its churches. Some have closed in recent years. Alaska Conference Historian Larry Hayden pointed out, "If you overlay the map of Alaska over the map of the lower forty-eight, Alaska goes from the East Coast to the West Coast—and we have twenty-eight churches. It's a lot of territory to cover."[45] Not everyone wants to move to Alaska and stay, so recruiting pastors for a limited run can be more feasible, but it may not provide the continuity that the region needs.

IN CONVERSATION

Continued from page 37

Alaska Natives and the Earth's Riches

As described above, the mission focus on Alaska Natives was important, but because of economics and geographic access, much of the outreach focused on the hordes of miners, entrepreneurs, and settlers who came to Alaska in search of riches—or fleeing from disgrace or other problems in the lower forty-eight.

The gold rush began the cycles of economic boom and bust in Alaska—which have never really stopped. Denominations and missionaries shifted most of their attention to incoming white miners and settlers. Although the get-rich-quick strategy switched from gold to oil over the years, the Alaskan economy is still suffering because of low gas and oil prices. With the current emphasis on renewable energy, the gas and oil businesses may never be what they once were.

Historically, the issues related to indigenous peoples have been who controls the land, natural resources, and wildlife. Today, we must also ask who controls the climate?

Alaskan Native peoples may have survived only to face the greatest obstacle of all—global warming. Today, the oceans are not freezing as solidly. Polar bears are finding it difficult to find enough ice to allow them to hunt, and the people are suffering as well. Parts of Alaska are four or more degrees hotter than they were thirty years ago.[46]

Alaskan Land Matters

There were no wars or treaties with the Alaska Natives. All property division and control was instituted when Alaska became a U.S. state in 1959. When statehood was established, a clause in the legislation specified that statehood did not include any lands to which Alaska Natives had a title, but no one really knew what that meant.

Millions of acres had already been set aside for national parks—and 104 million acres had been established as belonging to the new state, but the statehood act did not say which 104 million acres. Once Alaska state officials started selecting their 104 million acres, the protests began.

Lower forty-eight government officials set their sights on Alaska, which they saw as a vast empty land. The Atomic Energy Commission wanted to experiment with low output atomic bombs there and also create a harbor using atomic bombs—which would have polluted grazing lands of caribou, the main source of food for native people in the region.[47] The Army Corps of Engineers wanted to build a huge dam—which would have wiped out several village sites and decimated nesting grounds for vast populations of wildlife.

The policies of assimilation cannot be relegated to nineteenth- and early-twentieth-century history. Too often today, indigenous cultures are romanticized until people come face-to-face with the complexities of Native American lives.[48]

This inability to even perceive the existence of indigenous Alaskans made the land claims ever more urgent. Throughout the 1960s there was major confusion, contention, and conversation. A government report entitled "Alaska Natives and the Land" described the parameters of actual land use that was used to establish permanent Alaska Native land, while other lands would be purchased from the native people by the U.S. government. The next challenge was to figure out how to make the money from these sales last forever rather than consider them just a one-time windfall that would quickly evaporate. In response, "native corporations" were established to help regional groups manage their financial resources to benefit all the members of each native region.[49]

Continued on page 45

The Rev. Carlo Rapanut, Superintendent of the Alaska Conference (2014–present)[50]

The Rev. Carlo Rapanut, superintendent of the Alaska United Methodist Conference, moved to Alaska directly from a United Methodist Conference in the Philippines. Rapanut served three appointments in the Philippines, including assistant to the bishop from 1998–2008. He served as senior pastor of The United Methodist Church of Chugiak in Anchorage starting in 2008, until he was promoted to conference superintendent in 2014.

Rapanut shares his experience of being a leader in Alaska:

People who come to Alaska have a sense of rugged individualism and want to do things differently. I come from the Philippines, so I too bring a unique perspective. When I arrived, a phrase I often ran into was "This is Alaska, we do things differently here." There is a certain sense of freedom—a frontier mentality. We are trying to use that freedom to explore new possibilities. We want to make it work. We are far from resources in the lower forty-eight, and we are often far from our extended families, so we have to band together and make the most of the limited resources.

Another issue we struggle with is transiency. The oil industry, the military bases create revolving doors and we see this in our churches. When we look at building capacity and sustainability, it is challenging since people are constantly leaving and arriving. We call it both a blessing and a curse.

In Chugiak, I served a bedroom community for Anchorage that was predominantly military. We reframed the revolving door, so we could have a more positive understanding. We decided we would not talk so much about not losing members. Instead, we are sending out missionaries from our congregations. We give them a candle and commission them to take whatever they have learned, some piece of wisdom to use in their next church and faith community. So we keep those connections.

Alaska also has a transience among our clergy. All of our clergy are members of other annual conferences. We ask for a minimum commitment of four years. If a minister serves under that, we prorate the family's move back to their home conference. For many clergy it is an adventure, a chance to do something very different, but it is also a sacrifice. They can be serving here and something happens with their family back home. They may miss family gatherings, and sometimes they do feel the need to leave early and it becomes a financial sacrifice, as well.

Decisions of the General Conference can impact Alaska in ways that the larger church does not always incorporate into their decision making. When the General Conference was considering an end to the guaranteed appointment, many of the clergy in Alaska started thinking

IN CONVERSATION

about going back to their home conferences right away to make sure they had an appointment before the guarantee was lifted.

As I travel the conference, many churches are struggling financially and they can't put a finger on why. Of course, the whole church has faced financial challenges with decreasing membership and the impact of the recession of the last decade, but Alaska also experiences this in our agency relationships.

As a missionary conference, the General Board of Global Ministries has had an administrative relationship with us. At one time, they recruited and trained clergy who would be commissioned as mission personnel to Alaska. They would pay for the move up and back. Each congregation and each clergy person had an Advance Special number and clergy would often itinerate in the lower forty-eight for a month or so each year to build relationships and salary support. Congregations built "sister church" relationships with other congregations in the lower forty-eight, and groups of church members would do exchanges or work in teams as seasons allowed.

Today, the arrangement has shifted. Even when I came to Alaska in 2008, I was given an Advance Special number, but today Alaska has only one Advance Special number for everything. Anyone who itinerates and raises money cannot give donors the feeling that they are giving to an individual pastor or congregation; they are giving to all the pastors

and congregations. That's good news for those clergy who are not that great at fundraising or do not have a sister church, and it is challenging for those who depended on that outreach to close the gap in their congregational budget.

Clergy still come from all over the lower forty-eight, but they are not trained and commissioned as missionary personnel, so the tenor of their placement is a little different, as well. Moving expenses are given to the Alaska Conference as a block grant, and we are expected to manage and pay for the moves of our clergy.

We in Alaska have changed, too. There came a point when some of our Alaska Native leaders asked us to consider not using the term "missionary" in our conference title. The Rev. Della Waghiyi, Ray Buckley, and the Rev. Charlie Brower pushed for dropping the "missionary" title, due to the negative association with missionaries that native people often have—both in Alaska and the lower forty-eight. So, although we have not requested formal changes at the General Conference level, in practice, we do not often call ourselves a missionary conference.

As Alaskan United Methodists, we are considering deeply what it means to be functioning as a missionary conference, even if we do not use the term out of respect for our brothers and sisters here in Alaska. We are exploring how we can adapt and continue to raise funds, build relationships, and manage our congregations.

There are conversations in the larger church about what it means to be a missionary conference. The United Methodist Churches in Alaska, with the exception of the Nome Community Church, are largely populated by people of Anglo descent. Some are urging missionary conferences to move into being a regular annual conference. Currently our only paid conference staff members are a superintendent and an assistant. We depend on lots of highly dedicated volunteers, and the Pacific Northwest Conference is a real gift to us as their treasurer works with us.

Alaska and the whole church are asking, "What does it mean to be in mission?" We are hoping that by understanding more about the Alaska United Methodist Conference people will want to be partners with us.

We have to weigh the history, the current need, and the future possibilities. For example, we have a small church in Dutch Harbor, in Unalaska, which is in the southwestern part of Alaska where the orphanage that became the Jesse Lee Home first started. When the children's home moved to Anchorage, the community initiated a church in the 1970s. Today, the local church model is not sustainable. The church in Dutch Harbor moved from having a full-time pastor to half-time and then to one-quarter time.

In this case, we are in the process of identifying the needs of the Unalaska community to see how best to be in mission. We could say, you can't pay your apportionments, so it is time to close, but we are not doing that because of the vital role that United Methodists can play in the community. We have an application in to the Church and Community Program to create a ministry to address vital needs of the people there. In some cases, we need to reframe how we look at ministry in these settings. A United Methodist presence is still important to the community, but maybe it's not a preaching ministry.

In contrast, we are going to close a small church in downtown Anchorage, which is also where our conference offices are housed. The reason is that the congregation has lived through its life cycle as a ministry in this neighborhood and is not able to make the shift. This community is very diverse— the demographics involve [various] language groups, ethnic groups—and we are looking at what the needs are. The new ministry could be a social ministry with a worship component, or a worshiping community that will have a social ministry component.

The issue for the whole denomination is how we treat small churches. Should they be closed if they are small and are not meeting their apportionments? If we close them, is there something else that is needed? Who are our partners in the area? What is the role of a missionary conference or district? There are many questions to ask and answer but fundamental to all of the questions is: What does it mean to be in mission?

IN CONVERSATION

The Rev. Charley Brower serves in the northern region of Alaska at Community United Methodist Church in Nome. The church "has a long history of leadership in this area starting with the merger of the "native" Methodist Church with the Federated Church, long before Native Alaskans were truly valued as God's children." [51]

The Rev. Brower is in a unique position. He is the only Alaska Native pastor appointed by The United Methodist Church and, as Conference Superintendent Carl Rapanut shared, "The people of the community are thankful to have one of their own." Brower serves in Nome, a town only accessible by air, and best known as the finish line of the annual 1,000-mile race along the Iditarod trail. Of the nearly 10,000 people who live in Nome and the surrounding area, about three-quarters are from native people groups. [52]

Brower describes his ministry, "Nome is a small community as far as the church is concerned. On an average Sunday, we have thirty-five or forty people at church. The work I do is more [about] the native community beyond The United Methodist Church. People from other churches call and want a home visitor because I am a native pastor. They would rather not have a nonnative pastor come visit because they think their home may not be clean enough, or they may have trouble with communication." [53]

In his time of service, Brower has become the spiritual leader for neighboring villages. When Brower says that he is the pastor of Community Church, young people express surprise and excitement, especially when he shares with them that they too can serve in mission and

ministry. There is currently an Alaska Native from the southern town of Sitka studying at St. Paul's Theological Seminary in Leawood, Kansas, who is interested in returning to Alaska to serve.

Brower has also been leading the development of "Giving Voice," a gathering of ecumenical, Alaska Native ordained ministers and certified laypersons who gather to discuss common issues that churches in rural Alaska have faced. They are exploring sustainable solutions for worship in rural villages, including home churches, common training for lay leaders, the inclusion of communities in the selection and support of local lay leaders, and cultural differences they have encountered when training indigenous persons for church leadership.

In a video produced by the Alaska Conference, Brower shares the theology of God's sacred creation and the communion found within a family as they work together to survive by hunting a whale.

> God is everywhere, this is his creation. It is our role to protect it, to keep it sacred. I am from Yupiak, the people from Northern Alaska. The people in my community are whalers. You catch a whale and it will feed you for months. Whaling is almost a spiritual thing. It is also very satisfying, even if we don't catch a whale, to be in fellowship with the family that's there. We spend several weeks together. It's a time of renewal of family ties. Spirituality for me is also being out in God's creation. To wonder and see how the greatness of the world is there. [54]

Continued from page 40

The historic Alaska Native Claims Settlement Act (ANCSA), which Congress passed in 1971 and President Nixon signed on December 17 of that year, granted Alaska Natives title to 44 million acres of historically used land in Alaska. The U.S. government paid $962.5 million in compensation so that Alaska Natives would not claim any title to the remaining land in the state. The 75,000 Alaska Natives were encouraged to enroll in one of the twelve regional corporations of their choice. Villagers could choose to form as many corporations as they wanted. Later, a thirteenth corporation was formed for natives living outside Alaska. This settlement was unlike anything that had ever been established for any Native Americans; it legitimized Alaska Natives as no other action had.[55]

Alaska Conference or Missionary District?

In 2016, a petition submitted to the General Conference through the leadership of the Alaska Conference was passed that allows a missionary conference to become a mission district with the support of the geographic annual conference in which it falls. The description of a mission district, provided below, sounds a lot like the description of a missionary conference, except that a mission district would be overseen by the district superintendent rather than the bishop.

> Petition Number: 60529-MH-¶415.4-G; Erbele, W. Terence—Ketchikan, AK, USA for Alaska UM Conference. Mission District Amend paragraph ¶ 415.4 as indicated following: ¶ 415.4. To form the districts after consultation with the district superintendents and after the number of the same has been determined by vote of the annual conference. Any district may be designated to be a mission district, and the district superintendent of that district, or his or her designee, shall be the agent in charge of the mission status, nature, and goals of the district.

> If there is a district missionary organization, or if funds for the district are anticipated from a conference organization, those bodies shall also be asked to approve the method of organization for a mission district. A mission district may be designated when any of the following conditions exist: 1) Membership opportunities and resources are limited and not likely to result in regular status for an extended period of time. 2) A strategic demographic, cultural, or language opportunity for serving a limited population is present. 3) It is expected that long-term sustaining funding from sources outside the district will be necessary to enable the district to exist. 4) The district is geographically located in a remote location from other districts of the annual conference. When any of these conditions exist, the bishop, in consultation with the congregational development area of the annual conference, may designate any district a mission district. The mission district may be organized in the same manner and have the same rights and powers as any district. Rationale: In some jurisdictions—Southeastern and Western—there are missionary conferences that might better be organized as districts; this change will make that possible without removing the mission status of such entities. What the full implication is of being a mission district would be left to the annual conferences to determine.

In the Alaska Conference's case, if it changed from being a missionary conference to a mission district, it would become a district of the Pacific Northwest Annual Conference, which is its geographic annual conference. It would retain the same right to recruit clergy from outside the district and conference that it has now, but its primary financial partnership would be with the geographic annual conference that helps support it. It remains to be seen what impact this option might have on all the missionary conferences.

IN CONVERSATION

In a conversation with missionary Fran Lynch, we discussed the current cultural context of mission and mutuality in mission.

One of the longest-serving missionaries in Alaska is Deaconess Fran Lynch, who is a church and community worker at Willow United Methodist Church in Willow, Alaska. She is in her twentieth year of ministry.

Fran shared that although the Alaska United Methodist Conference covers 586,000 square miles, the culture of working in Alaska is one of a "small conference." This is due in part to the isolation of the work. The geography of the land she serves in plays an important part in how she does ministry, as well as the people she serves.

Lay ministry has to be strong in this region since clergy families and other missionaries who come to serve in the Alaska United Methodist Conference are far from their own families, and in Fran's words have to "have a heart for ministry to serve in Alaska."

Unlike Fran, most folks see their assignment in Alaska as temporary, so part of their assignment is to cultivate strong lay leadership to carry on the work of mission and ministry after they leave. She explains:

As a church and community worker, I am here to help Willow United Methodist Church figure out how to meet the needs of the community. I do this by partnering with area churches, businesses, civic groups, and individuals not related to our church. This generates funds, volunteers, and leadership. Willow Recycling has touched a piece of the Willow community that was not in existence eighteen months ago. Ministry grows because we live open doors, open hearts, open minds. We share our resources, money, time, talents, and service in such a manner that others share their resources with us. This is a witness to how we live as the community of God's people. A few people have a conversation. Others are invited in. A plan develops, and action happens. We see results. Five loaves and two fish were shared. All were fed with twelve baskets left over. Welcome to the world of church and community ministry!

Because of the diversity of the geography and the immensity of the state, The United Methodist Church in Alaska has developed key programs to assist families in remote locations with food insecurity and emergency assistance.

A COMMENTARY

Della Waghiyi, an Alaskan Yupik, presents a handmade garment to Bishop Ruediger Minor in June 2001. The Rev. James Campbell holds a microphone to catch the soft-spoken Waghiyi's words. A UMNS file photo by Tim Tanton. Used by permission.

When an elder dies, a village does not just lose a person. When an elder begins a new life, a presence, a memory is taken away. It is not just a piece; it is an enormous portion of corporate, tribal thought that is irreplaceable. When the Rev. Della Waghiyi died, the church lost a credible person of faith, a rare theologian and a Native conscience.

Della Waghiyi saw the Alaskan April snow as a blanket for the birth of baby seals. She was a master skin-sewer, whose Yupik dolls graced museums, and who carved trumpeter swans of walrus ivory while sitting on the floor of her home. She tanned moose and sealskin by hand. When visiting New York, she loved the people of all races and ages, but missed seeing the sky. She told the stories of her people, singing and dancing with her hands, moving like dragonflies in July.

Della never wrote a book on theology. Yet, for many Native scholars, Della Waghiyi was considered a profound Native natural theologian. The formation of ideas, molded across the years of experience, would emerge cohesively after she became an elder. In humble, carefully chosen words, she would speak of God, leaving scholars scrambling to capture all of her words before she quit talking. She believed that her people knew God before missionaries, and sought to remind Native people that Native culture was a gift of God.

Native people often write and speak in the "passive voice," preferring the cultural imperative of not asserting self over others. Choosing the passive voice is not being passive. Della would listen seriously to everyone else before speaking. As an elder, she still saw her world as her responsibility and would ask the question, "What must I do with God's help?"

She saw the role of elders and older people as critical in effecting change, in villages as well as the church. To Della, God's work was God's work. It never occurred to Della to make something a denominational project. Behind many Native-related ecumenical projects in Alaska is the influence of Della Waghiyi pulling as many people as possible into ministry.

She reluctantly wrote a simple story of her life, "While I Have My Being." English words were sometimes difficult. St. Lawrence Island Yupik was not a written language until well into her life, and the Bible is still being translated. Della would often ask, "May I use my tongue?" She would pray in Yupik, the soft, rounded words accented by gentle clicking sounds. She would be released from English, and her spirit lifted. One felt that here was a soul who knew God intimately.

Presence of God

Yupik, like other Native peoples, live across international borders. Yupik people live in Alaska and Siberia, Russia. Della and her husband, the late Rev. John Waghiyi, had ministered among the Siberian Yupik in Russia. Years later, in her trailer in Anchorage, Della heard of the starvation of the Siberian Yupik. The elders and the very young were suffering. Many were forced to eat their sled dogs. Unable to eat, Della put down her plate and began to pray. She phoned her friend, the Rev. James Campbell, pastoring in Willow, Alaska, and asked for his help. They became the core for the founding of the Chukotka Native Christian Ministry, later Russian Far East Task Force, to help meet the immediate humanitarian needs of the Yupik and Chukchi peoples in Siberia.

With the joint effort of Moravians, Presbyterians and United Methodists, the programs they began provided fishing nets, outboard motors, job development, encouragement of traditional art forms, food, clothing, medical care and training for laypersons engaged in ministry. The Native American Comprehensive Plan gave the largest grant of its history toward the relief in Siberia. The credibility of the work established by Waghiyi and Campbell helped to establish new lines of communication with the Russian government in Siberia, opening avenues for humanitarian aid.

An elderly woman in a trailer in Anchorage set in motion events that changed history in a part of the world. Wherever Della was invited to speak, she traveled, telling of the needs of her people and sharing her culture and faith. She would speak of the presence of God, saying, "Amazing. Isn't it amazing?"

The Path to Ordination

The Book of Discipline of the United Methodist Church extends to missionary conferences, in the case of indigenous candidates, the same avenues of cultural discretion afforded central conferences. At age 78, Della Waghiyi, was asked if she would consider being a candidate for ordination. Without looking up, she replied, with a quiet voice, "I'll ask him (God)." Two and a half months later, she said simply, "Yes. It's OK."

Others did not see it so simply. Clergy serving in the Alaska Conference of The United Methodist Church are members of other conferences. Many clergy and one layperson opposed the ordination of Native people under the disciplinary discretion. They feared it would set a precedent accepting unqualified Native clergy in non-Native settings and financially obligate them to guaranteed appointments, minimum salaries and clergy benefits. Native people from across the country had attended the annual conference for Dellas's ordination. They would remember the discussions of that day as some of the most painful in their lives.

On a Friday evening, 2007, Della Singigpaghmi Waghiyi was ordained an elder in The United Methodist Church. She wore a white, hooded *cuspuk* in the Yupik style, spontaneously translating the liturgy of ordination and Word and Table in Yupik. She knelt on a caribou skin, like those that had covered the floor and walls of her driftwood home as a child. There was a polar bearskin on the floor near the altar. These were signs of the provisions and gifts of God for the Yupik people.

Small, and somewhat frail, she stood with the chalice of Christ, offering the lifeblood of Jesus. Many present had never received the words from a Native voice, and the Eucharist from Native hands. Although a few Alaskan Native people had been ordained in the history of The United Methodist Church, none had been ordained by the conference in Alaska. At 78, the Rev. Della Waghiyi became the first Alaskan Native woman ordained in the denomination. She was ordained and retired in the same service.

Alaska has the highest per capita statistics for abuse against women. The largest percentages of those are Native women, who are often seen as acceptable targets. At 78 years of age, Della Waghiyi, great-grandmother, grandmother, mother, auntie, friend, Yupik woman, wore a red stole.

On July 4, 2010, the Rev. Della Waghiyi, internationally known Yupik artist and cultural scholar, profound thinker and Christian theologian, the first Native person to be ordained in Alaska, the first Alaskan Native woman to be ordained in the denomination, crossed over into new life, where drums are beating, relatives are dancing with the movements of hands, and the Great Cloud of Witnesses are speaking Yupik, a language that God loves.

*Ray Buckley is the interim director of the Center for Native American Spirituality and Christian Study.

Copyright © 2006–2012 United Methodist News Service.

A COMMENTARY

Endnotes

1. For a vivid description of the work in the region, read pages 310–15 in *Alaska, and Missions on the North Pacific Coast* by Sheldon Jackson (New York: Dodd Mead & Co. Publishers, 1880), accessed July 27, 2016, https://books.google.com/books?id=moEUAAAAYAAJ&pg=PA302&dq=Fort+Simpson+Methodist+Church+mission+to+alaska+canada&hl=en&sa=X&ved=0ahUKEwjOioCL0JPOAhWNth4KHfZ1BycQ6AEIHjAA#v=onepage&q=Fort%20Simpson%20Methodist%20Church%20mission%20to%20alaska%20canada&f=false.

2. Larry Hayden, "History," Alaska United Methodist Conference website, accessed July 27, 2016, http://alaskaumc.org/?page_id=182.

3. Arlow William Andersen, "Norwegian-Danish Methodism on the Pacific Coast" (volume 19: page 89), Norwegian-American Historical Association, accessed December 5, 2015, www.naha.stolaf.edu/pubs/nas/volume19/vol19_5.htm.

4. "Klondike Gold Rush: The Perilous Journey North," Special Collections, University Libraries, University of Washington, accessed December 5, 2015, www.lib.washington.edu/specialcollections/collections/exhibits/klondike.

5. "The Klondike Gold Rush," Digital Collections, University of Washington, accessed December 5, 2015, https://content.lib.washington.edu/extras/goldrush.html.

6. Kenneth O. Bjork, "Reindeer, Gold, and Scandal" (volume 30: page 130), Norwegian-American Historical Association, accessed December 23, 2015, www.naha.stolaf.edu/pubs/nas/volume30/vol30_05.htm.

7. Andersen, "Norwegian-Danish Methodism on the Pacific Coast" (volume 19: page 89).

8. "Exploration and Settlement on the Alaska Coast," *Harriman Expedition Retraced*, PBS, accessed January 4, 2016, www.pbs.org/harriman/1899/exploration.html.

9. Albea Godbold and John H. Ness Jr, revised by Edwin Schell and Mark Schenise, "Table of United Methodist Church Annual Conferences, 1796–2015," General Commission on Archives and History, The United Methodist Church, January 1998, revised October 2015, www.gcah.org/research/former-annual-conferences.

10. "Ancient Archeological Sites in Alaska," Bureau of Land Management, accessed December 8, 2015, www.blm.gov/ak/st/en/prog/cultural/archaeology.print.html.

11. Andrew Curry, "Ancient Migration: Coming to America," *Nature: International Weekly Journal of Science*, May 2, 2012, www.nature.com/news/ancient-migration-coming-to-america-1.10562.

12. "Alaska Native History and Cultures Timeline," Alaska's Digital Archives, accessed December 8, 2015, http://jukebox.uaf.edu/site/jukebox-includes/vilda/timeline.pdf.

13. "1743–1867 Era of Russian Violence," Alaska Humanities Forum, accessed October 14, 2016, www.akhistorycourse.org/southwest-alaska/1743-1867-era-of-russian-violence.

14. "Sheldon Jackson," AlaskaWeb.org, accessed December 23, 2015, http://alaskaweb.org/bios/jacksonsheldon.html.

15. Jordan Craddick, "Pandering to Glory: Sheldon Jackson's Path to Alaska," master's thesis, University of Alaska Fairbanks, August 2013, accessed December 8, 2015, 17, http://doyonfoundation.com/static/files/Jordan%20Craddick%20thesis%20-%20Pandering%20to%20Glory%20-% 20Sheldon% 20Jackson-s%20Path%20to%20Alaska.pdf.

16. Ibid., 24.

17. Ibid., 58.

18. "1885: Alaska regions assigned to religious denominations," *Native Voices*, U.S. National Institute of Health, and Human Services, accessed December 8, 2015, www.nlm.nih.gov/nativevoices/timeline/366.html.

19. Jordan Craddick, "Pandering to Glory: Sheldon Jackson's Path to Alaska," 16–19. http://doyonfoundation.com/static/files/Jordan Craddick thesis - Pandering to Glory - Sheldon Jackson-s Path to Alaska.pdf.

20. Stephen W. Haycox, "Sheldon Jackson in Historical Perspective: Alaska Native Schools and Mission Contracts, 1885–1894," Alaskool, accessed June 22, 2016, www.alaskool.org/native_ed/articles/s_haycox/sheldon_jackson.htm.

21. Russell W. Estack, *The Aleut Internments of World War II: Islanders Removed from Their Homes by Japan and the United States* (Jefferson, NC: McFarland & Co. Inc., 2014), 58–59.

22. Larry Hayden, "Alaska's Comity Agreement," unpublished paper, 2009.

23. Robert Laird Steward, *Sheldon Jackson, Pathfinder and Prospector of the Missionary Vanguard in the Rocky Mountains and Alaska* (Boston: Boston University Press, 1908), accessed July 24, 2016, 364–65, https://archive.org/stream/sheldonjacksonpa08stew/sheldonjacksonpa08stew_djvu.txt.

24. Roxanne Willis, "A New Game in the North: Alaska Native Reindeer Herding, 1890–1940," The Forest History Society, accessed February 28, 2016, www.foresthistory.org/fellowships/willis.pdf.

25. Dianna Haecker, "Reindeer Herding Holds Great Future for Seward Peninsula," *Alaska Fish and Wildlife News*, October 2010, Alaska Department of Fish and Game, www.adfg.alaska.gov/index.cfm?adfg=wildlifenews.view_article&articles_id=484.

26. Nome Community Center, "About Us," accessed January 3, 2015, www.nomecc.org/about-us.html.

27. "Alaska Native Claims Settlement Act (ANCSA) 1971," Federal Indian Law for Alaska Tribes, University of Alaska Fairbanks, accessed July 27, 2016, https://tm112.community.uaf.edu/unit-3/alaska-native-claims-settlement-act-ancsa-1971.

28. Bea Shepard and Claudia Kelsey, *Have Gospel Tent Will Travel*, Alaska Missionary Conference of The United Methodist Church, Conference Council on Ministries, accessed December 20, 2015, 85, http://alaskaumc.org/wp-content/uploads/2011/07/Have-Gospel-Tent-Will-Travel-front-cover-to-page-106.pdf.

29. "Jesse Lee Home for Children: 1824 Phoenix Road," Seward Historic Preservation Commission, accessed January 4, 2016, www.cityofseward.net/hpc/historic_properties/jesse_lee_home.html.

30. Ibid.

31. Alaska Family & Child, "History," accessed June 22, 2016, www.akchild.org/our-story/history.html.

32. Raymond L. Hudson, *Family After All: Alaska's Jesse Lee Home, Volume I, Unalaska, 1889–1925* (Walnut Creek, CA: Hardscratch Press, 2007), "Chapter 30: The Pandemic of 1919," reproduced at "Jesse Lee Home, Alaska, and the Pandemic of 1919," *Grassroots Science*, accessed January 4, 2016 https://ykalaska.wordpress.com/2008/02/23/jesse-lee-home-alaska-and-the-pandemic-of-1919.

33. Ibid.

34. "Jesse Lee Home for Children," Seward Historic Preservation Commission.

35. "Benny Benson: An Alaska Kid Who Made History," Alaska Historical Society, accessed January 4, 2016, http://alaskahistoricalsociety.org/discover-alaska/kids-page/benny-benson-an-alaska-kid-who-made-history.

36. Gene Brown, "Life at Jesse Lee Home," Growing Up Anchorage, May 25, 2012 *growingupanchorage.com/2012/05*.

37. Aleut is the Russian name for the Unangan people.

38. "Evacuation and Internment, 1942–1945," National Park Service, accessed May 16, 2016, www.nps.gov/aleu/learn/historyculture/unangan-internment.htm.

39. "Evacuation and Internment, 1942–1945," National Park Service.

40. "Evacuation and Internment, 1942–1945," National Park Service.

41. Margaret Snider, *Joined and Held Together: A Children's Study on Missionary Conferences* (New York: United Methodist Women, 2016).

42. "History," AK Child & Family, accessed December 8, 2015, www.akchild.org/our-story/history.html.

43. Ibid.

44. Thom White Wolf Fassett, Alaska Conference superintendent (1984–1988) and member of the Iroquois Nation, telephone interview with author, February 20, 2016.

45. Larry Hayden, chair, Alaska Conference Commission on Archives and History, telephone interview with author, February 2016.

46. "Impact of Climate Change on Alaska Native Communities," Alaska Native Science Commission, accessed August 20, 2016, www.nativescience.org/pubs/Impact%20of%20Climate%20Change%20on%20Alaska%20Native%20Communities.pdf..

47. Norman Chance, "Project Chariot: The Nuclear Legacy of Cape Thompson, Alaska," Arctic Circle, accessed August 16, 2016, http://arcticcircle.uconn.edu/SEEJ/chariotseej.html.

48. "Being Indigenous in the 21st Century" Cultural Survival, accessed February 15, 2016, www.culturalsurvival.org/publications/cultural-survival-quarterly/none/being-indigenous-21st-century.

49. "Alaska Native Claims Settlement Act," Modern Alaska, Alaska Humanities Forum, accessed August 16, 2016, www.akhistorycourse.org/modern-alaska/alaska-native-claims-settlement-act.

50. The Rev. Carlo Rapanut, Alaska Conference superintendent, telephone interview with author, February 25, 2016.

51. "Community (NunaaqiGmiut) United Methodist Church—Nome, Alaska," accessed August 20, 2016, www.cumcnome.org.

52. "Quick Facts: Nome Census Area, Alaska," United States Census Bureau, accessed August 20, 2016, www.census.gov/quickfacts/table/PST045215/02180.

53. "Alaska Native Pastor," The United Methodist Church, September 11, 2014, www.umc.org/news-and-media/first-alaska-native-pastor.

54. Ibid.

55. Paul Ongtooguk, "The Annotated ANCSA," Alaskool, accessed August 16, 2016, www.alaskool.org/projects/ancsa/annancsa.htm.

56. Fran Lynch, deaconess and church and community worker in Alaska, telephone interview with Deborah Bass, April 2016.

57. Ray Buckley, "Native Theological Led by Faith, Work," The United Methodist Church, July 23, 2010, http://archives.gcah.org/xmlui/bitstream/handle/10516/2028/8538079.htm?sequence=1.

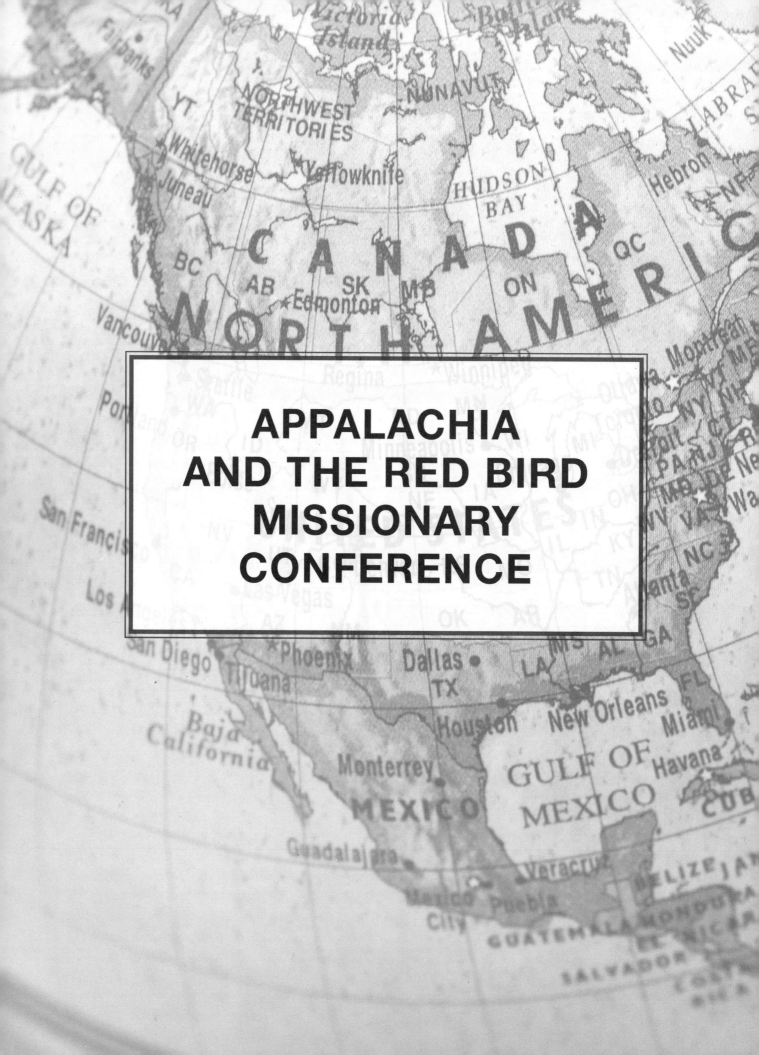

APPALACHIA
AND THE RED BIRD
MISSIONARY
CONFERENCE

CHAPTER 5

Appalachia and Alaska share a common trait in that they were first valued for their abundant wildlife for fur trading. Then gold drove immigrants to Alaska and coal dominated the economy in most of Appalachia. To this day, Appalachian coal is a national issue. With the downturn in coal usage, Appalachian town populations are dwindling and the people that remain suffer the effects of even greater isolation.

To understand the Red Bird Missionary Conference, it is critical to understand the larger context of Appalachia.

Coal Country

In the late 1800s workers from Scotland, Russia, Wales, Italy, and other countries flocked to Appalachia to do the backbreaking work of coal mining.[1] They worked twelve- to eighteen-hour days and often saw the sun only on Sunday.

A PBS *Frontline* special, "Country Boys," traced the poverty so many in Appalachia experience today to the 1870s, when white pioneers claimed small or large tracts of land in the mountains with seemingly unlimited reserves of forests. Later, industrialists from the east came and paid these landowners mere pennies per acre for both hardwoods and mining rights. They rigged the contracts so that the mountain dwellers would

pay the property tax while the big companies had the right to extract coal to satisfy the growing Industrial Revolution. The demand for coal was so great that coal-mining companies would build entire towns and then bring in the miners, bankers, managers, and retailers to fill them. They literally owned the entire town. As early as 1910, about 85 percent of the land in the Cumberland Plateau (an area that includes much of eastern Kentucky and Tennessee, and portions of northern Alabama and northwest Georgia) was owned by nonresidents.[2]

Miners earned good wages and benefited greatly from the coal industry until the Great Depression (1929–39), when everything ground to a halt. World War II revived the need for coal, but the price for this fuel was much lower and that shortfall came out of miner's wages. Coal extraction also became increasingly mechanized; instead of digging holes into mountains and bringing the coal out by rail, companies began to employ huge machines to deforest and raze entire mountaintops for coal. There was nothing the miners—or their communities—could do to combat these changes. Neither the coal industry nor the miners have recovered. In recent years, the focus on developing sources of clean, renewable energy has created further stress on this struggling region. Although the turn to clean energy

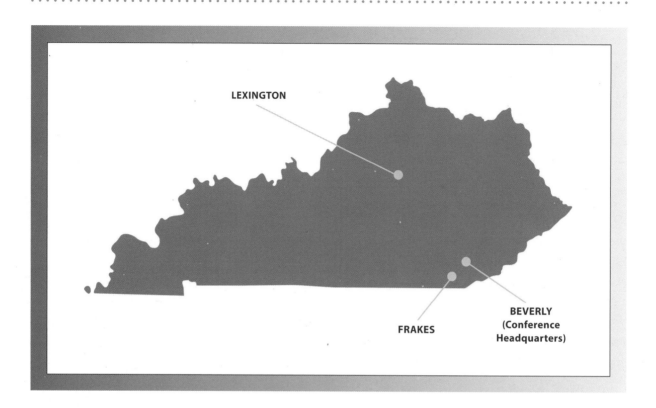

is ultimately good, the communities of Appalachia need a plan for supported economic growth to make up for the dwindling coal economy. Today, coal is quickly becoming a fuel of the past—but not before mining ravaged much of the Appalachian Mountains and surrounding valleys of this ancient and once pristine land.

Earlier this spring [1992], the federal government was poised to give a green light to the Big Branch Surface Mine in Pike County, Kentucky. The Central Appalachia Mining Co. planned to deforest and demolish several mountain peaks in order to excavate 7.3 million tons of coal—the technique known as mountaintop removal. The resulting debris would fill five nearby valleys, burying more than 3½ miles of streams under massive, sculpted piles of rocks.[3]

Appalachian resources continue to be a political and economic football in a game played by the powerful and rich. Coal mining was a lightning rod issue in the 2016 presidential campaign: Even though U.S. consumption of coal is going down, globally, consumption of coal is escalating, with China in the lead for sheer volume.

It remains to be seen if America has the willpower to create new jobs and new industries for economically depressed regions like Appalachia. Will the church make a difference?

Regional History

The Appalachian region covers over 200,000 square miles and stretches from southern New York to northern Mississippi.[4] Our focus in this study is on a small area of eastern Kentucky, called Red Bird. The major mission locations of the Red Bird Missionary Conference are near the Cumberland Gap—the primary gateway to the West that led to the Ohio River Valley, hotly contested land in the mid-eighteenth century desired by England, France, and Spain.[5]

France lost the French and Indian War in 1763 and the British consolidated their power. James Kenny, a Quaker trader with Native Americans of the region, recorded their reaction to the French handing over Native American land to the British. Delaware Chief Newcomer declared that "The English was [sic] grown too powerful and seemed as if they would be too strong for God himself." The Delaware Indians knew that peace between the French and the English was not good news for them.[6]

> British provocations only made matters worse: the arrogance of General Jeffrey Amherst, who referred to Native Americans as "pernicious vermin"; his desire to render Indians into defeated subjects rather than allies ("it is not my intention ever to attempt to gain the friendship of Indians by presents"); the occupation of French forts throughout the Ohio Valley; and especially the continual encroachment of British settlers into the region. Sir William Johnson, the British superintendent for Indian affairs, reported that even Mohawks—the oldest of British allies—felt themselves in "danger of being made slaves, and having their lands taken from them at pleasure." Native Americans throughout the West discerned a sinister British design to seize their land and render them impotent.[7]

In the meantime, settlers were not happy with policies that kept them from moving westward without restriction. First they rebelled against the British. Then, after American Independence in 1776, they resisted any restraints put on them by the U.S. government. In 1791, President George Washington placed a new excise tax on all liquors. A huge rebellion emerged in west-ern Pennsylvania, which included many former Revolutionary War soldiers as participants. They remembered the Boston Tea Party and demanded "no taxation without representation" one more time. Some even argued that they should align themselves with Great Britain or Spain and they created a flag of six stripes, one for each county represented in the rebellion. Although Washington sent a peaceful negotiator, he also mustered 13,000 troops from the Atlantic states and the rebels disbursed before the troops arrived. A key leader fled west to escape prosecution. Two men were convicted of treason and sentenced to hang, but Washington later pardoned them.[8]

Kentucky was less organized in their rebellion against the tax on liquors, but records show that 175 agitators were arrested over several years for their participation in the insurrection.[9] All of this is to say that settlers moving west viewed East Coast elites with suspicion; they also did not necessarily understand or follow the terms of the treaties that the government was making with First Nation leaders.

> "The right to unrestricted access of the Mississippi was the sine qua non of western loyalty," observes Andrew Cayton. "And many frontiersmen, particularly residents of Kentucky, were convinced that the United States was not interested in obtaining it." As American settlers poured into western lands, provoking Native reprisals, it was becoming imperative for the U.S. government to assert its sovereignty—or risk losing the region entirely. Nor was Spanish policy the only threat. Great Britain, still controlling key forts in the Great Lakes, was poised to sail down the Mississippi and take control of Spanish posts, including New Orleans, thus controlling access to the Gulf of Mexico. British officials, meanwhile, pursued overtures to alienated western settlers, who, ever more disenchanted with their government's policies, began to wonder if Great Britain might prove more solicitous. . . .

A national "separation," Thomas Jefferson warned in 1787, "was possible at every moment." [10]

The Cumberland Trail in Kentucky, long used by Native Americans, was shut down from 1754–63 during the French and Indian War. The 1783 Treaty of Paris, negotiated between Great Britain and the United States, not only ended the American Revolutionary War; it also designated land stretching from the Appalachian Mountains to the Mississippi River as Indian Territory. But the region that would become Kentucky, including the Cumberland Gap, was the first area to be retrieved by the U.S. colonies. [11] As the region was a desirable tool of war, commerce, and territorial expansion, it is not surprising that it was the first.

The famous explorer Daniel Boone traveled through the Cumberland Gap in 1769 and became enamored with the bounty and beauty of the area. In 1771, Boone and his group were joined by a significant hunting party and they hunted more prey than they could manage. They took home many pelts by boat but had to leave behind some 2,300 deerskins—which were ruined by the time they returned. [12] This is the kind of decadence and disregard for natural resources that became the hallmark of early settlers who believed in Manifest Destiny—that God had given them the right to the land and its resources. Even the mountains have not been safe from their destruction, as we see from the coal-mining practice of "mountain topping," which eliminates the need for tunneling by removing the entire mountaintop in order to extract coal.

Predictably, the Cumberland Gap continued to be a highly contested area. Although the Paris Treaty designated the gap part of Indian territory, it was considered extremely valuable by white settlers as it offered a passage through the Appalachian Mountains that could further their ongoing efforts toward westward expansion.

By 1800 the states of Kentucky, Tennessee, and Virginia claimed the area through the Cumberland Gap. After 1840 a weekly stage carried freight, mail, and passengers and gave the area a prosperous commercial appearance. During the Civil War [1861–65], the gap changed hands four times as the North and South fought for control of this strategic gateway. Initially considered part of Kentucky, and therefore under Union control, the first troops to occupy the Cumberland Gap were Confederate forces under the command of Brigadier General Felix K. Zollicoffer. Union commander Brigadier General George W. Morgan took the "American Gibraltar" on June 18, 1862. Morgan did not remain at the gap, however, and Confederates reoccupied the area immediately. After a year of inactivity, Union forces reappeared, and Major General Ambrose E. Burnside demanded and received unconditional surrender. The gap was not seriously threatened again during the remainder of the war. [13]

Although the pass was considered the gateway to the West, the Appalachian Mountains were both a destination and an obstacle for westward immigrants. People of European descent—Scotch-Irish, English, German, Polish, Portuguese, Spanish, French, as well as descendants of both slaves and free Africans made up the tapestry of people who settled in the region. [14] These families put down roots in the valleys and hills of the region, where they often became very isolated, a situation that caused them to develop unique speech patterns. [15]

Linguistic research sometimes claimed this speech revealed remnants of Elizabethan English, but such research was often in response to the denigrating caricatures of mountain people seen in cartoon strips like "Li'l Abner," first published in 1934, and the television show *The Beverly Hillbillies*, which aired from 1962–71.

These caricatures of Appalachians emerged out of a culture of extreme poverty, which was a product of the concerted domination of land and resources, such as coal, by business and industrial interests. The caricature of the ignorant hillbilly worked in the interest of those in power.

The War on Poverty

The dire economic straits of the Appalachian region came into sharp relief when Kentucky became the poster child for poverty leading up to President Johnson's War on Poverty, which he declared in his 1964 State of the Union address. Johnson shepherded more than two hundred pieces of legislation through Congress to help more than 37 million impoverished Americans. Senior citizens gained the most.

Johnson's policies are considered the largest expansion of social safety net programs in history. He created Medicare and Medicaid, which provided health care to millions of low-income people and seniors. He also launched the Head Start early education program and made housing available for low-income people. On top of that, Johnson successfully expanded funding for K–12 education, passed the Voting Rights Act and provided money for artists through the National Endowment for the Arts. [16]

COUNTY ECONOMIC LEVELS IN THE APPALACHIAN REGION
Effective October 1, 2016 through September 30, 2017

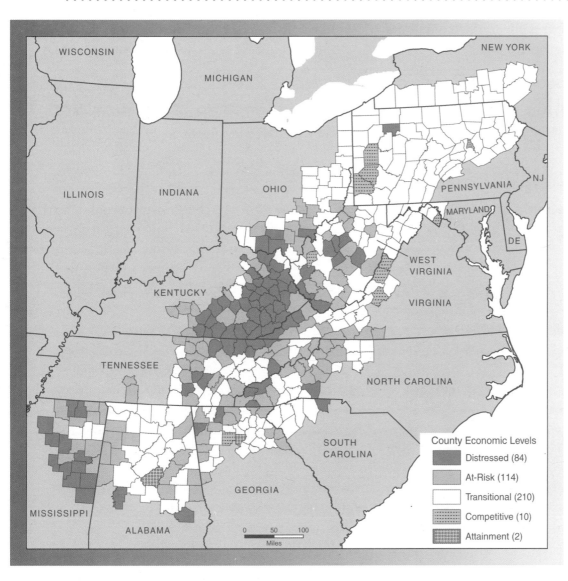

Created by the Appalachian Regional Commission, March 2016

Data Sources:

Unemployment data: U.S. Bureau of Labor Statistics, LAUS, 2012-2014

Income data: U.S. Bureau of Economic Analysis, REIS, 2014

Poverty data: U.S. Census Bureau, American Community Survey, 2010-2014

County Economic Levels
- Distressed (84)
- At-Risk (114)
- Transitional (210)
- Competitive (10)
- Attainment (2)

Despite these efforts, poverty in Kentucky diminished only slightly over the decades that followed the War on Poverty. Today, the people of Appalachia are still living with high rates of poverty, but they can receive government assistance through disability payments, child welfare, food stamps, health insurance through Medicare and Medicaid, and some job training; however these services only scratch the surface. In 2014, when the fiftieth anniversary of the War on Poverty rolled around, broadcasters visited Kentucky again and found that the poverty rate had only gone down slightly.

A map of poverty rates throughout Appalachia, created in 2016 by the Appalachian Regional Commission (see previous page), reveals that poverty patterns have changed little, and that Kentucky suffers from some of the highest rates of poverty throughout the region.[17]

It does not appear to be a coincidence that the counties in Kentucky where gas and oil extraction are occurring match the areas suffering from poverty almost exactly (see map below).

During the 1980s, there was public criticism of government-sponsored social programs designed to allow impoverished families to get on their feet again, and these programs are now viewed with suspicion by many Americans. Nonetheless, these government safety-net programs are still helping people to survive the harsh economic realities of Appalachia. Church ministries, like those of the Red Bird Missionary Conference, are also critical to the well-being—and even survival—of many families, as well.

The success or failure of federal programs to combat poverty in the region need to be understood in the context of Kentucky state politics.

REPORTED OIL AND GAS PRODUCTION FOR KENTUCKY COUNTIES IN 2015
(latest year for which production data are publicly available)

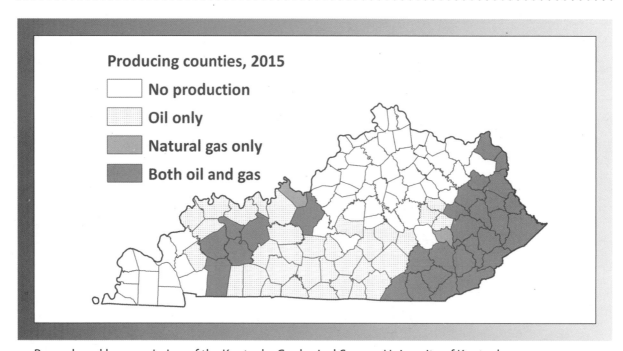

Reproduced by permission of the Kentucky Geological Survey, University of Kentucky.

Kentucky has a history of political cronyism going back to its early years that affects property ownership and political power to this day.

> Though land in the new Commonwealth of Kentucky was quickly claimed, it wasn't fairly or equally distributed among its many new inhabitants. By 1810, eastern Kentucky had become known as a "poor man's country," where some 57 percent of households were landless (the number was as high as 74 percent in some of Kentucky's eastern counties). Statewide about 25 percent of landowners possessed more than three-fourths of all the land, and one-quarter of the land was owned by only 21 individuals. The wealth of these "backcountry elite," as they were called, grew and grew, while the fortunes of their neighbors, mainly self-sufficient yeomen farmers, stagnated or dwindled. [18]

Kentucky has long been a playground for the rich and famous, who frequent the Kentucky Derby and the horse country of western Kentucky, while the eastern sector has been the stomping ground of industrialists who have exploited the poor.

The ever-widening gaps in wealth were exacerbated by the corrupt and undemocratic nature of Kentucky's early government. For the first half of the nineteenth century, most government responsibilities were administered by justices of the peace—those county magistrates who were appointed for life by the governor and oversaw everything from property assessment to tax collection, as well as the settlement of civil and criminal disputes. All other county officials served at their discretion. According to two University of Kentucky historians, Dwight Billings and Kathleen Blee, remnants of this early system of patronage and political clientism persist in many communities in Kentucky to this day, forming one of the region's major stumbling blocks to economic improvement. [19]

The Red Bird Missionary Conference Serving the Community

The Red Bird Missionary Conference is located in the middle of this impoverished region. Such poverty is not new to the region, and the economic impact caused by the area's geography and politics has not changed much over the centuries. Mission in the current geographic area goes back almost a century, but the predecessor organization to the Red Bird Missionary Conference can be traced back to 1955:

> The Kentucky Missionary Conference was formed in 1955 when the Cumberland Mission District (former United Brethren) and the Red Bird Mission District (Evangelical) were brought together and given status as a Missionary Conference in the 1956 Discipline of the General Conference of the Evangelical United Brethren Church. Following the union with the Methodist Church in 1968, the churches of the Cumberland District moved into the Louisville Conference. In order to avoid confusion with the pre-existing Kentucky Conference, the name of the Red Bird Mission District was changed to Red Bird Missionary Conference. Several former Methodist Churches have been added. At the formation of the Conference, Red Bird Mission, Red Bird Clinic and Henderson Settlement became institutions of the Red Bird Missionary Conference. The Bennett Center of London joined the Conference in 2003. [20]

The Red Bird Mission is located in Red Bird Valley, an isolated area where three counties converge. As in many counties in eastern Kentucky, there are few educational and medical services other than in the county seats. The Red Bird Missionary Conference provides services to more than 14,000 people a year, which are supported by United

Methodist mission giving. Education, health and wellness care, economic opportunities, and community outreach programs are offered to the entire area. A thrift store, GED classes, farming and gardening programs, the Family-to-Family food pantry, and children, youth, and senior services make all the difference to people who depend on the Red Bird Missionary Conference. [21]

The Red Bird Christian School

In 1921, two teachers and a United Evangelical pastor named John J. DeWall arrived in the Red Bird Valley at the invitation of the community. DeWall served the mission until his death in 1928. [22] The main purpose of the mission was the establishment of a school, therefore DeWall started the Red Bird Settlement School for primary and secondary students. In 1921–22, the school's first year, six high school students and ninety-five elementary students attended. The next year a dormitory was opened. [23]

Red Bird Christian High School was founded in 1921 by the Evangelical Church. It was one of the original "Settlement Schools" of Appalachia. The Settlement School movement in Appalachia began in the late 19th and early 20th centuries. During this period the nation became intensely aware of the economic and educational deprivation of the Southern Highlander via numerous published newspaper and magazine articles. John C. Campbell's book, *The Southern Highlander and His Homeland*, was published in 1921 and issued a clarion call for Church and private organizations in the North and Mid-West to come into the mountains and establish boarding schools and other mission projects.

Red Bird Settlement School early on became a boarding high school serving mountain people from isolated communities spread far and wide. The school and dormitories epitomized high quality secondary and college preparation

education. Missionary teachers streamed into the school through the years making it a school comparable to the elite private boarding institutions of the northeast.

The Evangelical Church soon united with the Brethren Church to form the Evangelical United Brethren Church (EUB). In 1968, the EUB Church united with the Methodists to become today's United Methodist Church. [24]

The school continued to grow and, in 1952, a gymnasium was added. Then, in May of 1981, a fire destroyed the school building and gym. A temporary school was set up in Queendale to accommodate the displaced students, and shortly thereafter, the school merged with Jack's Creek Elementary School.

The current school building was dedicated in 1983, and the school was renamed the Red Bird Mission School in 1988 when it separated from the public school system; from then on it was funded by the Red Bird Missionary Conference along with income-based tuition. The school changed names again in 2012 to Red Bird Christian School to better reflect the school's nature. [25]

Today, the school's budget is close to four million dollars and it has about one hundred employees with an average salary of about $24,000. [26] There are around three hundred students, many of whom live in the dorms due to the remoteness of their family homes. [27]

The Red Bird Clinic and Community Outreach [28]

Lydia Rice, RN, was the first medical director of the Red Bird medical services that began in 1922. Dr. Harlan Heim joined the staff in 1926 and, in 1928, the first hospital was built in Beverly. For many years, medical staff made house calls on horseback. In 1975 Red Bird Hospital, later renamed the Red Bird Mountain Medical Center, was incorporated and became the third agency of the Red Bird Missionary Conference. The hospital operated until 1986 when in-patient services were discontinued for economic reasons. In 2000 Red Bird Mountain Medical Center was renamed the Red Bird Clinic, Inc. to better reflect its activities; today it operates as an outpatient ministry.

Red Bird Clinic also has a dental clinic staffed with one dentist, two dental assistants, and a part-time dental hygienist. The medical clinic is staffed by two doctors and a physician's assistant, along with other medical personnel.[29]

The Red Bird Missionary Conference's community outreach ministries seek to meet the needs of the whole person. Their programs are a significant part of the overall ministry. In addition to the school and health services, Red Bird's community outreach ministries include community housing improvement, craft marketing, a thrift store, adult education and job skills training, an early childhood development program, food and baby pantries, summer and afterschool youth enrichment programs, the Grow Appalachia gardening project, a senior citizens center, homebound services, and home-delivered meals.[30]

The clothing and craft ministries increased in scope after moving into the current facilities on Queendale Center. Churches host craft shows and sales and Red Bird Mission Crafts bring in handmade items created by artists at the Red Bird Mission.[31]

Providing care and support for senior citizens is also a key community outreach of Red Bird Mission. The DeWall Senior Citizens Center opened in 1991 and the Red Bird Elderly Housing apartments opened in 1996.[32]

The Work Camp Program at Red Bird Mission hosts more than 2,500 volunteers every year. Work Camp staff and participants support the mission and community by performing simple home repairs for low-income community residents and maintenance for mission buildings and grounds.[33]

On Becoming a Missionary Conference[34]

Deaconess Betty Letzig shared her insights and observations through a telephone interview and correspondence in February 2016. Betty Letzig served as staff in the National Division of the Board of Missions, which became the General Board of Global Ministries in 1968, when the Evangelical United Brethren Church (EUB) and the Methodist Episcopal Church (MEC) were joined. Shortly after, the Red Bird Missionary Conference became a part of Betty's portfolio, and for many years she provided administrative and programmatic support to the new Red Bird Missionary Conference.

The fate of Red Bird Mission hung in the balance when the union between the EUB and the MEC took place:

> Red Bird Mission had been fully supported by the EUB Church largely through an annual, denomination-wide Women's Society of World Service offering called the KYN Offering that was designated for the three major EUB mission projects in Kentucky Red Bird Mission, Ybor City in Florida, and the New Mexico Group Ministry— three expansive mission programs that operated in some of the most economically challenged counties in the United States.
>
> After the union, these three mission programs became three among hundreds of programs sponsored by the General Board of Global Ministries. Significant attention was given to maintaining the

unique character of these programs, but from the beginning, it was difficult to explain why these three programs received more funding than the average United Methodist mission project.

From the Red Bird perspective, the loss of direct funding when the union occurred was devastating and confusing. How could a small denomination like the EUB fully support mission projects and a large denomination like the Methodists not be able to continue that? The uncertainty of Advance Specials[35] replaced the certainty of an annual offering. To help in the transition, a full-time development officer was employed by Red Bird.

Red Bird stood out because it was a comprehensive mission program unto itself with evangelism through local churches, and outreach through the school, hospital, dental clinic, and senior citizens program.

The union in 1968 and efforts to support Red Bird came in the midst of great turmoil in the country and the dismantling of the segregated Central Jurisdiction as part of the terms of the union. Across the country, historically black churches were being merged into predominantly white conferences and their opportunities for leadership and attention to their congregations diminished. It was not surprising that competition for resources grew.

The bishop of the Kentucky Conference understood the importance of maintaining the Red Bird mission work as an identifiable entity within the new denomination because of its historical relationship with the EUB since 1921. The EUB did not have a conference in Kentucky. The Red Bird Mission related directly to the EUB national offices in Dayton, Ohio.

If the Red Bird Mission had become a part of the Kentucky Conference, the ordained elders serving Red Bird would have been assigned to churches in the larger Kentucky Conference because there was a significant shortage of elders in Kentucky. Because it was a smaller conference, pastors assigned to Red Bird would not have been elders and they would mostly not have had an understanding of the historical nature of the work. The entire area would have been receiving less experienced and less trained pastoral leadership.

Becoming a missionary conference gave them the autonomy to retain ordained pastors, and to recruit clergy from across the denomination to meet the needs of the congregations and communities they served. As a missionary conference they could appoint their own clergy to local churches, and appoint elders to other projects in the conference such as the Red Bird School, the hospital, and Henderson Settlement, which had come from the Methodist side to become a part of the missionary conference at the time of the union.

Today, it is amazing that the Red Bird Missionary Conference has retained all of the programs except the hospital, which is now a clinic. They continue to expand their other programs through senior housing, and Henderson has expanded via additional outreach locations. Red Bird continues with crafts and a clothing store, while Henderson Settlement now includes a program for maternal health, and additional sites beyond their original area.

Continued on page 67

In a conversation with Marilyn Osbourne, the United Methodist Women president in Red Bird, she shared the following:

Red Bird Missionary folks are mission-minded folks. Missionaries and volunteers who come in to serve, live, and work side by side with the local folks and encourage the locals to become involved in their communities. They exemplify true mutuality in mission by forming deep relationships and partnerships.

Because of the generosity of work teams who have come into the area year after year now, local folks see themselves as being able to give back to others within our denomination both within the United States and outside. Congregations participate in Volunteers in Mission Teams, in addition to serving on teams that assist persons who are affected by natural disasters. This is a mission-minded conference. Because we have been helped, we want to help others. In some cases, members who are unable to go on teams will contribute financial support to team members.

We celebrate the reopening of the Red Bird boarding school. This has helped to break down ethnic boundaries since these young people participate in community and church life. Students from all over the country and the world are attending the school and the racial divide is coming down within the churches and community.

Current ministries important in Red Bird include food security, clean water, and senior housing.

Those involved in Red Bird Missionary Conference ministries know the work is valuable. The programs that emerged at the Henderson Settlement where Marilyn serves as a member of the board of directors are summarized on its website:

The building vacated by the closure of the high school in 1976 was made into a community center. Fellowship lunch, Outreach services, tutoring and adult education saw their formal beginnings. The closing of residential childcare in 1990 freed resources to expand community development programs and begin new ones. The work camp program took on home improvement. A senior citizens center opened, providing transportation, access to health services, and a social outlet. Recycling of aluminum cans began the hopes of reducing the area's litter problem. Youth ministries grew to offer activities year-round. Recreational programs are now provided for the general public. A former residential childcare home was remodeled into a day care center as a service to working families. [37]

IN CONVERSATION

The Rev. Farley Stuart, Conference Superintendent of the Red Bird Missionary Conference [38]

IN CONVERSATION

Conference Superintendent Farley Stuart reflects on the Red Bird Missionary Conference, which he describes as one of the most comprehensive mission efforts of The United Methodist Church in the United States.

If the Red Bird Missionary Conference did not exist with its twenty-three churches, mission institutions, and partnerships, the southeastern Kentucky Appalachian communities would not be served. "We make disciples for Jesus Christ in the heart of Appalachia," he explained.

Historically, this region has been one of high unemployment and little opportunity. The mountains cause isolation, making basic life services difficult to reach. In the rural areas, it can take an hour to drive to the grocery store, bank, or hospital. Industries are very few in this area. Therefore, many people are left unemployed or are forced to travel extensively to work. Even with new roads and better transportation, the seclusion the mountains create still lingers, leaving many people isolated from work and basic services.

The Red Bird Missionary Conference helps ease the need and the isolation through its churches and mission institutions. The churches work to teach and train local leaders as well as to provide long-term discipleship. Church and outreach workers work diligently with the children through camp and youth groups. The Appalachian Local Pastors School (ALPS) is also provided to train local pastors to serve in churches. Of the current pastors in the conference, one is a product of the ALPS program

and grew up in the Red Bird Missionary Conference. The Rev. Jack Short, an ALPS graduate, says, "I have received 'missionary help' from the Red Bird Missionary Conference, and now I want to work within a conference that has done so much for me, to serve others in my native land as I have been served."

The mission institutions of Red Bird offer a wide range of ministries. Henderson Settlement provides community care and outreach ministries: agricultural, craft, and clothing ministries, elderly and children's ministries, and work camp and retreat ministries. Red Bird Mission and Clinic provides a medical clinic, dental clinic, laboratory, and x-rays; elderly, family, and children's ministries; housing repair, craft and clothing ministries; the Red Bird Christian School and an early childhood development program.

There are thousands of individuals across the United States who have partnered with the Red Bird Missionary Conference by volunteering, sending supplies, and through covenant relationships with the permanent mission workers serving here. One of the key partners is the Kentucky and Red Bird partnership. Our two conferences are intentionally working in partnership with each other through personal relationships and prayer; sharing gifts and services through a needs list for churches, outreach centers, and agencies; volunteer and work teams; and covenant relationships through the Advance Special. It takes the support of the entire United Methodist Church to meet our needs.

Continued from page 64

As for the future of the Red Bird Missionary Conference, it may go the way of other missionary conferences and be absorbed into its surrounding geographic conference. Red Bird's needs have not gone away, but would the local churches be better served by the larger Kentucky Conference, or would they miss the benefit of having clergy assigned from any conference in the United States? Would mission projects like Henderson Settlement House, the Red Bird Clinic, and the Red Bird Christian School function as well if they were simply among the many mission projects of the church that have to raise the bulk of their own funding from grants, donors, and fees? Will people remember and value the historic nature of the complete mission program that was established by the EUB? History is important but the administrative needs of the conference, the missionary conference, and Global Ministries are also a factor. Time will tell.

Endnotes

1. David A. Fahrenthold, "Rousing the Ghosts of Appalachia," *Washington Post*, October 3, 2007, www.washingtonpost.com/wp-dyn/content/article/2007/10/02/AR2007100202172.html.

2. "A Short History of Kentucky/Central Appalachia," *Frontline*, PBS, accessed December 30, 2015, www.pbs.org/wgbh/pages/frontline/countryboys/readings/appalachia.html.

3. John McQuaid, "The Razing of Appalachia: Mountaintop Removal Revisited," *Environment 360*, Yale University, May 12, 2009, e360.yale.edu/feature/the_razing_of_appalachia_mountaintop_removal_revisited/2150.

4. "The Appalachian Region," Appalachian Regional Commission, accessed May 23, 2016, www.arc.gov/appalachian_region/TheAppalachianRegion.asp.

5. François Furstenberg, "The Significance of the Trans-Appalachian Frontier in Atlantic History," *The American Historical Review*, accessed December 12, 2015, http://ahr.oxfordjournals.org/content/113/3/647.full.

6. Philip Ranlet, "The British, The Indians, and Smallpox: What Actually Happened at Fort Pitt in 1763?" Hunter College, accessed February 24, 2016, https://journals.psu.edu/phj/article/download/25644/25413.

7. Furstenberg, "The Significance of the Trans-Appalachian Frontier in Atlantic History."

8. "The Whiskey Rebellion," People & Events, PBS Thirteen, accessed August 20, 2016, www.pbs.org/wgbh/amex/duel/peopleevents/pande22.html.

Endnotes *continued*

9. "The Whiskey Rebellion," History of Spirits in America, Distilled Spirits Council of the United States, accessed December 29, 2015, www.discus.org/heritage/spirits/#7.

10. Furstenberg, "The Significance of the Trans-Appalachian Frontier in Atlantic History," accessed October 16, 2016, http://ahr.oxfordjournals.org/content/113/3/647.full.

11. W. H. Perin, J. H. Battle, and G. C. Kniffin, *Kentucky: A History of the State* (Louisville, KY: F. A. Battey and Company, 1887), accessed December 29, 2015, 106, https://books.google.com/books?id=0dc_AAAAYAAJ&pg=PA106&lpg=PA106&dq=kentucky+treaty+1768&source=bl&ots=wIE3KmeNIs&sig=gEJWhnVjVFyHn50PJRn-kSvs77M&hl=en&sa=X&ved=0ahUKEwiG-r2Gh4LKAhVLyWMKHeIbCHsQ6AEIKDAC#v=onepage&q=kentucky%20treaty%201768&f=false.

12. Ibid., 114.

13. Rebecca A. Vial, "Cumberland Gap and Cumberland Gap National Historical Park," *The Tennessee Encyclopedia of History and Culture*, accessed December 29, 2015, https://tennesseeencyclopedia.net/entry.php?rec=338.

14. "Smoky Mountain Speech," *American Varieties*, PBS, accessed December 30, 2015, www.pbs.org/speak/seatosea/americanvarieties/smokies.

15. Michael Montgomery, "The Scots-Irish Element in Appalachian English: How Broad? How Deep?," University of South Carolina, accessed December 30, 2015, http://artsandsciences.sc.edu/engl/dictionary/articles/ScotchIrishElement.pdf.

16. Leigh Ann Caldwell and Dan Merica, "America's Longest War," *CNN Politics*, January 8, 2014, www.cnn.com/2014/01/08/politics/war-on-poverty-50-years.

17. "County Economic Status in Appalachia, FY 2017," Appalachian Regional Commission, March 2016, www.arc.gov/research/MapsofAppalachia.asp?MAP_ID=116.

18. "A Short History of Kentucky/Central Appalachia," *Frontline*.

19. Op cit, "A Short History of Kentucky/Central Appalachia."

20. "IV. Historical Statement and Constitution and By-Laws" in "2011 Journal: One Person, One Mission, One Kingdom," *Journal of the Red Bird Missionary Conference of The United Methodist Church*, April 29–30, 2011, http://redbirdconference.org/library/143-RBMC_Journal_2011_-_online_without_directory.pdf.

21. "Red Bird Mission, serving the needs of Eastern Kentucky," Facing Hunger in America (blog), November 6, 2010, http://facinghungerinamerica.blogspot.com/2010/11/red-bird-area-of-kentucky-is-deep-in.html.

22. Roberta Schaeffer, *The Story of Red Bird Mission* (Nashville: Parthenon Press, 1980), 10.

23. "History," Red Bird Christian School, accessed May 16, 2016, http://redbirdchristianschool.org/?q=content/history.

24. "About Us," Red Bird Christian School, accessed August 20, 2016, www.redbirdchristianschool.org/?q=content/about-us.

25. "History," Red Bird Christian School.

26. Red Bird Christian School: 2013 990 IRS Form, Guidestar.org, accessed December 23, 2015, www.guidestar.org/FinDocuments/2013/610/674/2013-610674373-0aabc7e2-9.pdf.

27. "Red Bird Christian School," *Boarding School Review*, accessed January 2, 2016, www.boardingschoolreview.com/red-bird-christian-school-profile.

28. The material from this section is taken from: Margaret Snider, *Joined and Held Together: A Children's Study on Missionary Conferences* (New York: United Methodist Women, 2016).

29. "Red Bird Clinic," Red Bird Missionary Conference, Inc., accessed May 16, 2016, www.redbirdconference.org/red_bird_clinic.php.

30. "Red Bird Mission," Grow Appalachia, accessed May 16, 2016, https://growappalachia.berea.edu/partner-sites/red-bird-mission.

31. "Check List for Hosting a Craft Show," Red Bird Mission, accessed May 16, 2016, www.crafts.rbmission.org/Crafts_Checklist.pdf.

32. "Monthly Mission for December—Red Bird," *Peoples UMC News* (blog), November 22, 2006, http://peoplesumcnews.blogspot.com/2006/11/monthly-mission-for-december-red-bird.html.

33. "Work Camp," Red Bird Mission, accessed May 16, 2016, http://rbmission.org/work-camp.

34. Betty Letzig, deaconess, telephone and email correspondence with author, February 2016.

35. The Advance is an official program of The United Methodist Church for voluntary, designated, second-mile giving. Annual conferences, districts, local churches, and organizations, as well as individuals and families, may support mission programs or mission personnel with their financial gifts. More information about The Advance is available online: www.umcmission.org/give-to-mission/the-advance.

36. Marilyn Osbourne, United Methodist Women president, Red Bird Missionary Conference, telephone interview with Deborah Bass, April 2016.

37. "About Us/Our History," Henderson Settlement, accessed October 26, 2016, www.hendersonsettlement.com/aboutus_history.php.

38. Farley Stuart, conference superintendent of the Red Bird Missionary Conference, telephone interview with Deborah Bass, April 2016.

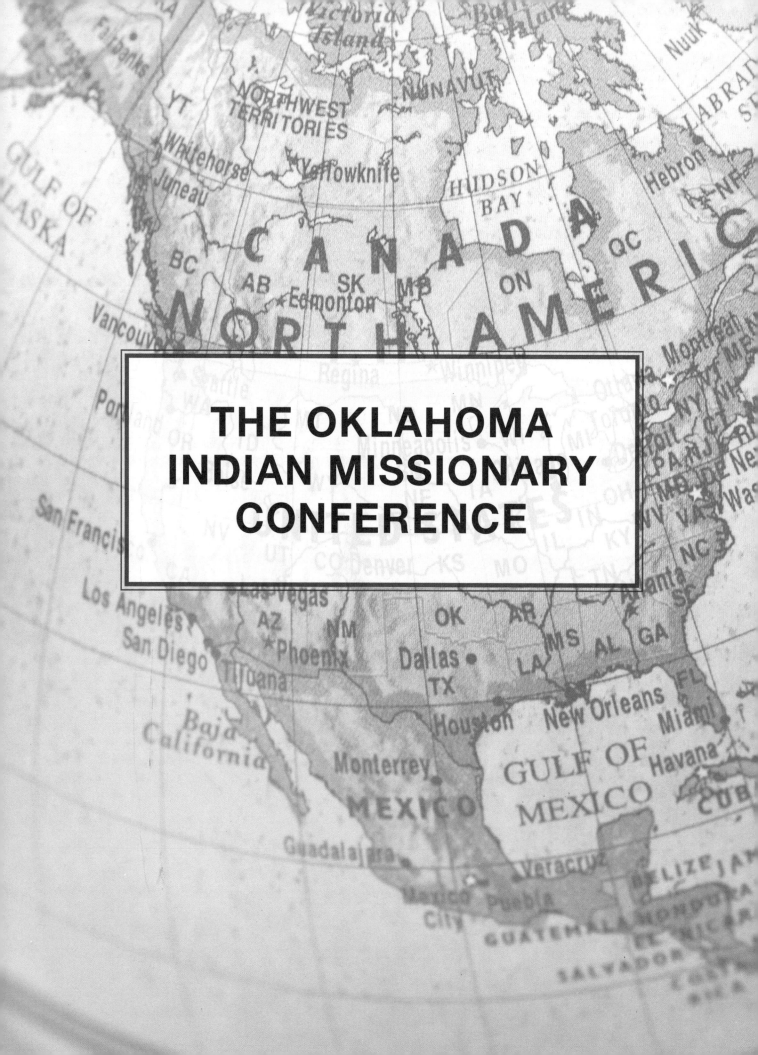

THE OKLAHOMA INDIAN MISSIONARY CONFERENCE

CHAPTER 6

Shrinking Indian Territory and Forced Removal

By the close of the colonial period, Native Americans had been largely forced out of the colonies, and the French and Indian War (1754–63) resulted in the Treaty of Paris, which pushed many native peoples west of the Appalachian Mountains. Five years later, in 1768, white "pioneers," who were either ignorant of the 1763 treaty or simply disregarded it, pushed through the Cumberland Gap onto the Indian Reserve.

After the American Revolutionary War ended in 1783, the boundary along the Appalachian peaks that separated the colonies from Indian Territory was officially revoked, and by 1789, the newly formed United States had completely subsumed the land that was formerly the "Indian Reserve."

In 1803, twenty years after the end of the American Revolution, the U.S. government sealed the deal on the Louisiana Purchase, acquiring approximately 827,000 square miles of land west of the Mississippi River from France—for the bargain price of less than three cents per acre. The westward surge expanded.

A U.S. military map demarcating U.S. states and the location of territorial forts from 1815–45 (see next page) tells the story of the country's westward expansion, driven by the ideology of Manifest Destiny. We can see clearly from this map that up until 1845, the Southwest was still a part of Mexico, although some of this territory was in dispute between Mexico and Texas, and later, the United States.

Within a generation, most settlers believed that only the territory west of the Mississippi was Indian Territory. The term did not indicate a relegation of land to the Native Americans, however; it merely suggested that Native Americans also lived in this territory, so if you were a settler in this region, you might face conflict. As the settlement of the western frontier proceeded in the 1850s, native peoples began to be squeezed further west into an Indian "strip" that ran from Nebraska to Oklahoma. In one more generation, that "strip" was reduced to Oklahoma and, by the end of the nineteenth century, the Oklahoma Indian Mission began to emerge. The process involved brutal wars, forced marches, broken treaties, and the genocide of native peoples.

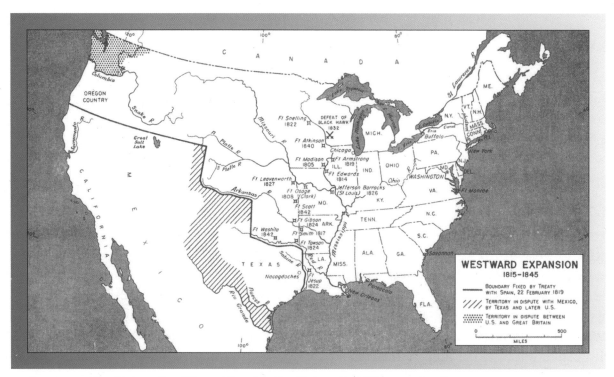

Courtesy of the University of Texas Libraries, The University of Texas at Austin.

In 1830, Andrew Jackson signed the "Indian Removal Act" which gave the U.S. President the power to remove Indians from their lands and give them lands west of the Mississippi. By 1837, the Jackson administration had removed 46,000 Native American people from their land east of the Mississippi, opening 25 million acres of land to white settlement and to slavery.[1]

Known as the Trail of Tears, this campaign is a heart-breaking example of the sort of theft and brutality perpetrated by the U.S. government on Native Americans in this era. Most members of the Cherokee, Creek, Choctaw, Chickasaw, and Seminole nations, known as "the Five Civilized Tribes," were forced to walk or travel by other precarious means from the Southeast to Oklahoma, a journey of approximately 1,200 miles.

As white farmers moved into Cherokee land in the southeastern United States, some Cherokees made the decision to migrate west on their own in the early 1800s. By this time, the Cherokees, like the rest of the Five Civilized Tribes, had acclimated themselves to the farming practices of the white settlers. In 1821, Sequoyah had created an alphabet of the Cherokee language and soon the tribe was publishing the *Cherokee Phoenix*. One article reported:

An 1826 survey showed that the Cherokee people (somewhat more than 13,000) owned 22,000 head of cattle, 7600 horses, 46,000 pigs, 726 looms, 2488 spinning wheels, 172 wagons, 2943 plows, 10 sawmills, 31 grain mills, 62 blacksmith shops, 8 cotton machines, 18 schools, and 18 ferries.[2]

The book *Georgia's Rome: A Brief History* also notes that the Cherokees owned 1,560 black slaves.[3] They had adopted many of the practices of white culture, but the white settlers still did not want to share land with the Cherokees.

White resentment of the Cherokee people continued to build, reaching a breaking point following the 1829 discovery of gold in north Georgia— Cherokee land. Thousands of gold diggers flooded the area. Backed by the Indian Removal Act, Georgia took possession of the land in 1830 and redistributed it through a land lottery.[4]

The Cherokees were U.S. allies at the 1814 Battle of Horseshoe Bend who had saved Maj. Gen. Andrew Jackson's life and the lives of his troops. Yet, it was Jackson who authorized the Indian Removal Act of 1830. Over the next decade, tens of thousands of Native Americans from the Five Civilized Tribes were "removed" from the southeastern United States through Jackson's Indian Removal Act. The Cherokee were among the last to leave and were forcibly removed by federal troops. U.S. senators Daniel Webster and Henry Clay spoke out against this forced removal of the Cherokee from their ancestral lands. The Rev. Samuel Worcester, a Congregational missionary to the Cherokees, took the State of Georgia to the U.S. Supreme Court to fight for the Cherokee's right to maintain ownership of their land. He won the case, but he and most of the other missionaries paid a dear price.

The Trail of Tears

Both the State of Georgia and President Andrew Jackson defied the U.S. Supreme Court's ruling in the *Worcester v. Georgia* case. Georgia's legislature passed a law making it illegal for whites to live on Cherokee land without obtaining a license and promptly arrested Worcester and others who were with him. They appealed to the Supreme Court again and were released, only to be arrested a second time. This is Worcester's account of his second arrest, along with eleven Methodist and Baptist missionaries, after which they were forced to march on foot to prison and bound by shackles.

Early on Friday morning July 8, I with my guard joined Sergeant Brooks at . . . the house of a near neighbor and rode then ten miles to where Col. Nelson was. There I found the Rev. Mr. Trott, a Methodist missionary who has a Cherokee family and a Cherokee by the name of Proctor. Proctor was chained to the wall of the house by the neck and had another chain around his ankle. He had been arrested on Tuesday on the charge of digging for gold, chained the first night by the ankle only, the second and third by the neck to the wall and to the ankle to Mr. Trott. Mr. Trott was arrested on Wednesday and taken on horseback about ten miles to where Col. Nelson then was. He had been before arrested and was under bonds to answer at Court for the offence of residing in the nation without license and now was taken again, and having committed the second offence by returning to his family while the cause was pending. On Thursday, he and Proctor were marched on foot 22 miles to the place where I found them, Proctor being chained by the neck to the wagon.

[Section where Worcester appeals to his captors to consider his sickly wife and infant—to no avail.]

We were then marched on foot 22 miles to the same place from which Mr. Trott and Mr. Proctor were taken the day before. Proctor again chained to the wagon. We had proceeded about three miles when we met Messrs. McLeod and Wells, Methodist clergymen not residing within the charter of Georgia. With leave of Col. Nelson, they turned and rode along some distance in our company. In conversation, Mr. McLeod asked Mr. Trott whether he had been chained the preceding night, and being answered in the affirmative, asked if it were according to the law to chain a prisoner who manifested no disposition to escape. Mr. Trott said he thought not, but that we ought not to blame those under whose charge we were as they were obliged to act according to orders. Mr. McLeod remarked, "It seems they proceed more by orders than by laws." This gave offence. A few words had passed between Mr. McLeod and some of the guards when Col. Nelson rode up and being told of the remark asked Mr. McLeod where he resides. He replied, "In Tennessee." Col. Nelson with a curse ordered him to "____ off." Mr. McLeod turning his horse said "I will sir, if it is your command" but added hastily as he afterwards said, "You will hear from me again." He was then riding away when the Col. ordered him to halt and then to dismount and lead his horse along in the rear. He then enquired of Mr. Trott whether this was one of their circuit riders. Mr. Trott answered, "Yes." Mr. McLeod's horse was then taken from him and delivered to Mr. Wells and he was declared a prisoner and ordered to walk on with the rest. For a short distance, Brooks compelled him to keep to the center of the road through mire and water threatening to thrust him through with the bayonette if he turned aside. In the meantime, he was heaping upon all our heads a load of tremendous curses and reviling missionaries and all minsters of the Gospel in language which for profanity and obscenity could not be exceeded. The word of our Savior he turned into ridicule—Fear not—said he tauntingly, Fear not, "little flock, for it is your Father's good pleasure to give you the kingdom." The manner in which these words were uttered did not prevent me at least from rejoicing in the consolation they afford. Brooks was the chief speaker and exceeded all though some others joined him in his reviling.

[Section where Mr. Wells, turns around to check on Mr. McLeod. He catches up to Col. Nelson and Wells becomes a prisoner, too.]

I know not what offence Mr. Wells had given unless in conversation with me, he had expressed strong disapprobation of the policy of the State of Georgia and the course pursued by the Executive of the United States. . . . .

At night the four prisoners were chained together by their ankles in pairs. Sometime after we lay down, a small detachment arrived with Doctor [Elisur] Butler. He had been arrested at Haweis [Mission] on the preceding day. After crossing a river, three or four miles from home, a chain was fastened by a padlock around his neck and at the other side to the neck of a horse . . . The horse was kept walking at a quick pace and [when] . . . the horse fell . . . Dr. Butler was considerably hurt, but the soldier more, having two ribs broken. . . .

. . . When they lay down, the prisoner was chained to his bedstead by the ankle . . . The next day they had 35 miles or more to travel. Dr. Butler wore the chain on his neck but was no longer fastened to a horse. [5]

Excerpted with permission from Voices from the Trail of Tears, *edited by Vicki Rozema, published by John F. Blair, Publisher; www.blairpub.com.*

In the end, Worcester recanted and begged for clemency because he saw no hope for their cause.

They had entered prison knowing that "the faith and justice of our nation were at hazard," and left realizing that [the] nation's pledge to protect the Cherokees had been "broken, and an act of flagrant robbery . . . was committed upon a defenseless people, with the sanction of our national authorities." Ultimately, they conceded, "there was no longer any hope" that they could help the Cherokee people. [6]

The U.S. government convened a small and unauthorized group of Cherokees to sign the 1835 Treaty of New Echota, which gave ancestral land of the Cherokee nation to the United States. The treaty, signed by about one hundred Cherokees, relinquished all lands east of the Mississippi River in exchange for land in Indian Territory and the promise of money, livestock, various provisions, tools, and other benefits.[7]

Chief John Ross, a man of Scottish and Cherokee descent, fought the treaty. He was determined to keep the Cherokee land through peaceful and legal measures. Elected principal chief in 1928, Ross learned the law and went to Washington, D.C., many times to plead the tribe's case in Congress and eventually turned to the Supreme Court. In fact, most Cherokees opposed the New Echota treaty. Although Ross' appeal to the court was successful and the court decided in favor of the Cherokees, Jackson ignored the ruling and used federal troops to force almost all of the approximately 15,000 Cherokees off of their southeastern homeland.

The Cherokees who signed the Treaty of New Echota also signed their own death warrants, since the Cherokee Nation Council had earlier passed a law calling for the death of anyone who gave up tribal land. Once these Cherokee arrived in Indian Territory, most lost their lives.

Under orders from President Jackson, the U.S. Army began rounding up the Cherokees and surrounding tribes in the summer of 1838. Some were loaded onto boats that traveled the Tennessee, Ohio, Mississippi, and Arkansas Rivers into Indian Territory. Others preferred to walk more than 1,000 miles rather than trust the leaky boats. Many were held in prison camps to await their fate.

An estimated 4,000 Cherokees out of 15,000 died from hunger, exposure, and disease over the course of the journey. Some Methodist missionaries walked the Trail of Tears alongside the Cherokees and other native peoples they were in

mission with. And an entire church building was dismantled by a Cherokee community and carried with them to Oklahoma to be rebuilt.[8]

Today, members of the Oklahoma Indian Missionary Conference (OIMC) are quick to remind other United Methodists that Native Americans brought Methodism to Oklahoma; they assert that it was not Oklahoman Methodists who evangelized the Cherokees and other nations. These early Native American Methodists faced deep bitterness among the nations towards Christianity as it was also used as a means of "civilizing" Native Americans; Creek Indians forbade their members from adopting Christian religious practices by force of whipping. Eventually, that changed.

The Cruel March of Manifest Destiny

The U.S. domination of Native American nations and their land continued to expand. James Polk, who became president in 1845, was cut from the same cloth as Jackson. He was a vocal advocate of Manifest Destiny ideology, and his campaign was based on two goals: to annex Texas as a slave state, and to conquer the disputed land controlled by Mexico. He had his way.

> After a clash in late April 1846 between American and Mexican troops in the area, Polk requested and received a declaration of war from Congress. Within sixteen months, U.S. forces drove deep into Mexico, capturing Mexico City in September 1847. In the Treaty of Guadalupe Hidalgo, the United States imposed a Rio Grande border for Texas and paid $15 million to Mexico for the territories of California and New Mexico.[9]

By 1861, just before the Civil War, the U.S. map looked more similar to today's map, only the state of California extended all the way down the Baja Peninsula.

In November of 1864, during the final throes of the Civil War, Col. John Chivington and approximately seven hundred soldiers brutally attacked a Cheyenne village called Sand Creek, in southeast Colorado, that had a peace agreement with the U.S. government in place. During this attack, which came to be known as the Sand Creek Massacre, more than five hundred women, men and children, were killed and mutilated. [10]

This event was central to the service of repentance that took place at the 2012 General Conference of The United Methodist Church. Chivington was a Methodist minister who had been talking of "a war of extermination" before he perpetrated this massacre. [11]

The government commission that investigated the massacre recommended the reform of the Bureau of Indian Affairs (BIA), which was infamous for skimming resources intended for Native Americans, who were now wards of the state living in reservations under treaty agreements. The commission recommended a policy of kindness to quell the ongoing violence, saying the government should use "the hitherto untried policy in connection with Indians, endeavoring to conquer by kindness." [12]

It is telling to hear the accounts of these actions from other denominational perspectives. The following report is from a Catholic perspective:

> To put the policy [Grant's Peace Policy] into effect, the government parceled out Indian agencies to the religious denominations then at work among the Indians. By this time, the various Protestant societies had, for the most part, dropped out of Indian missionary work, focusing their efforts overseas. The Roman Catholic Church, however, had expanded its work among Native Americans. For this reason, Catholic clergymen expected to be given control of thirty-eight Indian agencies.

Their expectations were unfulfilled. The Indian Department assigned only seven agencies to the Catholics. Fourteen agencies were turned over to the Methodists, ten to the Orthodox Friends, nine to the Presbyterians, eight to the Episcopalians, six to the Hicksite Friends and five to the Baptists. Naturally, the Catholics were disappointed. [13]

A letter-writing campaign to government officials ensued, first to increase the number of Catholic agencies, then just to get one knowledgeable person in Washington to be an advocate for Catholics and Indian rights. But throughout its history, the bureau's guiding principle had been to keep Native Americans away from the Catholic Church. [14]

> Quakers, Methodists, Episcopalians, and all the other Protestants, fighting for the religious liberty of their own groups on the reservations, made no move to grant so much as a hearing to the Indian religions. The record of the Catholics was no better. They criticized Protestant bigotry and called for freedom of conscience, but that freedom did not extend to native religions, which were universally condemned. The missionaries were not interested in the Indian's right to maintain and defend his own religion. By religious freedom they meant liberty of actions on the reservations for their own missionary activities. [15]

It was the Southern Methodists who organized most of the work in the Indian Territory, but there were Northern Methodists who were in the midst, as well. When the schism between the southern and northern branches of the Methodist church occurred over slavery, there was deep dissension but, in the end, the vote went for Indian Territory to join with the MEC (South). Even some tribal nations that had come from the Southeast had acclimated themselves to the white culture—including the ownership of slaves.

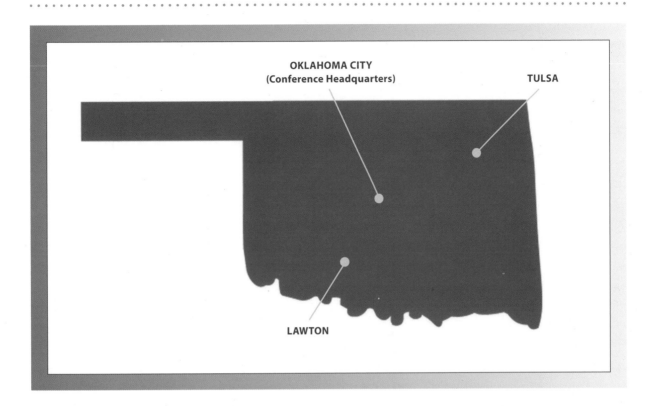

OKLAHOMA CITY
(Conference Headquarters)

TULSA

LAWTON

The Birth of a Conference

The complex layers of ministry and mission were driven by divisions based on settlers, slavery, and race. In the early 1800s Methodists preached at Pecan Point near the Arkansas border, and schools such as Asbury Manual Labor School, Choctaw Academy, and Bloomfield Academy served the Creek, Choctaw, and Chickasaw nations. The Creeks punished Christian preaching with flogging, but eventually, converts among the Creeks reduced the resistance to Christian preaching.

The 1844 organizational meeting of the Indian Mission Conference was at Riley's Chapel in a Cherokee area of Oklahoma. The conference was dominated by whites and, despite protesting the schism, the conference voted to align with the Methodist Episcopal Church (South). After the war, the Methodist Episcopal Church (North) worked among the Wyandotte Indians and established an Indian Mission for the territory in 1880, which, by 1889 became a full conference. The Methodist Protestant Church also actively ministered to the Indians, mostly in rural areas. In 1887 the Methodist Protestants organized an Indian Mission Conference that became the Fort Smith–Oklahoma Conference in 1916. [16]

With a growing white membership, in 1906, the Indian Mission Conference of the MEC (South) in Indian Territory met at Tulsa and ceased to exist. Instead, it became the Oklahoma Annual Conference. The churches serving Native Americans were neglected. After repeated complaints, in 1918, they formed the Indian Mission to serve "distinctly Indian congregations." [17]

Even through the merger of North, South, and Protestant Methodists in 1939, the Indian Mission of Oklahoma was ruled by the white Oklahoma Conference, until 1972, when it became the Oklahoma Indian Missionary Conference. For the first time, they voted at General Conference, and could ordain their own clergy and own property. [18]

The Rev. Dr. David Wilson, who has been the Oklahoma Indian Missionary Conference (OIMC) superintendent since 2002, recounted stories of OIMC's struggles to become a separate missionary conference in the 1960s and 1970s. During one interview, he discussed the late Tom Roughface, member of the Ponca and Chickasaw tribes, who was pivotal in the fight to establish the OIMC:

> While the [Civil Rights] demonstrations, occupations, and armed standoffs were going on across the nation, Methodist Native Americans were working just as hard to occupy their own conference. It was time for the OIMC to become a reality.

> There were people who strongly resisted the idea of the Indian Mission becoming a missionary conference. As a missionary conference, we would manage our own conference; our conference would own our own property, ordain our own clergy, and be free to invite clergy from across the church to come and serve here. Resistance came from some of our own who felt like they could get promotions in the white conference more easily. Some people thought we could never manage on our own. Resistance was strong at General Conference in 1972. Our resolution was even being blocked by keeping it off the legislative calendar. Finally, at the very end of General Conference, we were able to get it to the floor and it passed. We

became a Missionary Conference. Bishop Woodie White, an African-American leader, was chair of the Commission on Religion and Race and was a key part of a team that made this happen.

> I remember Tom Roughface kept and made notations in the 1972 hymnal for General Conference in which he wrote, "OIMC gained the status of Missionary Conference." The 2016 General Conference is the same place where [it was] 40 years earlier; that was accomplished. The first action on returning home in 1972 was retrieval of the church and parsonage property titles. We began ordaining our own people and rejoiced in the work our ancestors had done to bring us this far.

> The 1960s and 1970s were turbulent years for African Americans, but they were also turning points for Native peoples, as well. [19]

During this turbulent time, the American Indian Movement (AIM) mobilized occupations and demonstrations to get the United States to live up to its treaties with Native Americans. Ronald Bacigal, professor of law at the University of Richmond, summarized AIM's actions in that era:

> From November 1969 until June 1970, AIM participated in the occupation of the abandoned federal penitentiary on Alcatraz Island in San Francisco Bay. The occupation was based upon a long forgotten law that provided American Indians with first claim to any "surplus" federal land. AIM militantly pursued this reclamation policy by following the Alcatraz occupation with the takeover of an abandoned Coast Guard station on the Great Lakes. AIM established a camp at Mount Rushmore as a symbol of Indian claims to the Black Hills while also sponsoring a demonstration to transform Thanksgiving Day into a National Day of Mourning at Plymouth, Massachusetts. [20]

Their most well-known action took place in 1973 at Wounded Knee, on the Lakota Pine Ridge Indian Reservation in South Dakota. This was the site of the Wounded Knee Massacre, on December 29, 1890, when a clash between federal troops and the Sioux resulted in 150 Native Americans being killed; nearly half were women and children. In this AIM-organized protest against centuries of violence toward and oppression of Native Americans, Dennis Banks, Russell Means, and more than two hundred Sioux and other Native Americans used the Methodist church on the Pine Ridge reservation to stage a takeover and hostage situation that lasted seventy-one days. It cost the lives of two native activists and paralyzed one FBI agent through gunfire.[21] When the standoff was over, more than one hundred native people were brought to trial. Some of the trials were held in Lincoln, Nebraska, where the trial judge was a prominent white member of The United Methodist Church. The site of the battlefield where the Wounded Knee Massacre took place has since been designated a National Historic Landmark, and, in 1990, both houses of the U.S. Congress passed a resolution formally expressing "deep regret" for the massacre.

Superintendent Wilson also reflected on the current challenges faced by the Oklahoma Indian Missionary Conference:[22]

Today, as it has always been, we face financial challenges. We need fair salaries for our pastors and to provide educational opportunities so they can become full elders when they [are ready]. OIMC is unique among the missionary conferences because we supply our own pastors. Red Bird and Alaska Conferences draw pastors from across the country, but we do not. We even supply staff to other conferences. Fawn White and her brother Woody are from OIMC and are working as United Methodists in the community of Nome, Alaska. Fawn started as a US-2 missionary[23] through the General Board of Global Ministries.[24]

Our congregations are producing leaders for our own people and for The United Methodist Church. We have eighty-seven churches with strong lay and clergy leaders who are committed to making disciples for Christ and transforming the world. We invite others on our journey. Although we get some support from the General Board of Global Ministries, most of our support comes from the General Commission on Finance and Administration as well as the Oklahoma Conference. We are working hard to fund an endowment to replace diminishing income from church agencies. We want to secure the future for our congregations and communities.

Although many conferences are closing churches, we are opening churches. When the Oklahoma Conference closes a church, they call us to see if there is a Native American community of Methodists who would like to establish a church there. This partnership has been a gift to all of us. It expands our presence to other Native American communities. In addition, we are always looking for where we can be in ministry—even outside our conference. As a missionary conference, we are not restricted and even now have churches in Kansas, Missouri, and Texas. It gives us the latitude we need to grow. Right now, a third of our leaders are lay ministers who have other vocations or are retired; a third are trained local pastors; and a third are full elders. Our strength is our belief as native people. We are proud of who we are.

Some of our churches incorporate Native American spiritual practices of sweat lodges, drums, and dances; others use less obvious native practices, but the songs that came with them on the Trail of Tears, the long services, and deep relationships are all signs of the old ways made new in a Christian context. Choctaw and Cherokee would not have had the same spiritual practices such as sweat lodges, so we don't come in only one style of worship or in being Native American. For some

Continued on page 82

Interview with Anita Phillips, executive director of the Native American Comprehensive Plan[25]

IN CONVERSATION

Anita Phillips who is a Cherokee, shared her reflections as someone who did not grow up as a United Methodist but now makes it her home faith community and provides leadership to the whole church as the executive director of The United Methodist Church Native American Comprehensive Plan.

I became a United Methodist twenty-five years ago as a young single parent and joined a small OIMC church in the Cherokee nation boundaries. I was looking for something good for my family. I grew up in a Native American and Christian environment. My mother was Pentecostal and my father practiced Keetoowah traditional Cherokee faith.

United Methodism was a good fit for my family. It was not high pressure or doctrinaire, and it provided vacation Bible school and hospitality—there were always cookies or food. I was not raised with doctrine other than knowing that wherever there was a cross, there were caring people.

The small Cherokee church I joined had a group of United Methodist Women. They taught me what the Christian walk was like in The United Methodist Church. I became very active in United Methodist Women and those women were my mentors and role models. Lay women were important for the younger generations in the church.

I have a lot of respect for the intellectual contributions of United Methodist Women to the whole church. I came into the Oklahoma Indian Missionary Conference without knowledge of United Methodist ways and polity, but the women knew. I absorbed so much. Then I felt a call and went to seminary after having worked as a social worker for twenty years. My master of social work degree fit in well with the caring profession of the ministry.

I have served several Native American churches and became a district superintendent. For the last eight years, I have been the executive director of the Native American Comprehensive Plan of The United Methodist Church. This is one of the six racial-ethnic plans that The United Methodist Church recognizes as being in special relationship to Native Americans, black churches, Latinos, and Pacific Islanders, Koreans, and other Asian language groups.

I serve OIMC and the rest of the Native Americans across the church. They may be in existing churches and native communities, which may not be Methodist or Christian but are part of the Native American community. The Comprehensive Plan offers the hope of Jesus Christ and the gospel in as many places as possible. The Native American Comprehensive Plan and the Strengthening the Black Church for the 21st Century program are under the umbrella of Discipleship Ministries. The Hispanic/Latino, Pacific Islanders, Korean, and

Asian-American Language Plans are overseen by the Global Ministries offices.

This year, I am privileged to be the alternate to the General Conference for OIMC. Within OIMC we have thirty-nine Native American nations represented. Missionary conferences take into account language, context, history, and socio-economic status as related to The United Methodist Church. As Native Americans we are at the bottom of the economic ladder. One thing OIMC does well is ministry with the poor. The majority of our people are at or below poverty; it makes it difficult when you are trying to support an elder.

Our survival is connected to mobilizing other bodies in The United Methodist Church to invest in us. The equitable salary compensation of United States churches is a good example. As a missionary conference we have the independence to make decisions for our conference. For example, we can set the base minimum salary for ministers in the OIMC lower than other conferences. That means local churches whose members are impoverished are not as burdened by the salary of the pastor, but it also means it is difficult for us to attract clergy.

Our bishops have worked hard to make our ministries more feasible. Bishop Bruce Blake helped us as we struggled with pension obligations, and Bishop Robert Hayes Jr. has worked with our superintendent, David Wilson, to create an endowment that makes it more possible to pay clergy fairly, and to

help candidates and lay pastors get the education they need. Our annual gala is hosted by our conference and is partially responsible for our improved standing for our clergy and superintendent.

In my twenty-five years as a member of The United Methodist Church I have seen a lot accomplished in OIMC. I have always been an optimistic person. We are dealing with the same issues that the rest of the church is dealing with. Those challenges are layered with our own contexts and worldview as Native Americans. I would say our challenges have made us sharper, and brought forth gifts that we didn't even know we had.

In the big picture of the whole church and the Native American plan, we don't want to be known as doing mission TO native peoples. We are drawing the churches attention—The United Methodist Church and the whole Christian church—to the contributions and the gifts and graces God has poured into Native American people. We are lifting up the depth of experience God is revealing through native ceremonies as well as Christian practices. God has gifted Native American people—all our relations —with a particular spirituality and a journey from which we can all learn. There is much to be appreciated. Even though we may live in poverty, native peoples are not always on the receiving end of mission. God has invested gifts in Native American peoples that are to be shared with the world.

Continued from page 79

though, many of the traditions were lost because Christian missionaries told them that they could not be Christian and practice Native American spiritual ways. Many would not be comfortable with burning cedar, sage, tobacco, and sweet grass, traditional Native American rituals.

Earlier this year, I was invited to preach at one of our oldest United Methodist churches in Oklahoma in far Southeast Oklahoma. The church, Bethel Hill United Methodist Church, was established on the top of the small mountain in the community of Bethel, by a group of Choctaw Methodists who were a part of the forced removal to Indian Territory in the early 1830s.

The Mississippi Conference began evangelizing among the Choctaws at the present-day site of the Mississippi Choctaw reservation near Philadelphia, Mississippi, as early as 1824 and a greater effort began in 1827, establishing a good number of Choctaw Methodists. As a result of this effort, many Choctaws converted to Christianity and to the Methodist Church. One of the first things these communities of Choctaws did after the Trail of Tears was to establish Methodist churches, with Bethel Hill Church being among the first.

While various English songs are sung at the church, Choctaw hymns are a big part of the life of this small Methodist church. Many of the members there are still fluent Choctaw speakers and one can see that Choctaw culture and life is an integral part of the congregation. The pastor is full-blood Choctaw and uses both Choctaw and English in her preaching as do persons who lead various parts of the service.

This congregation is certainly distinguished as a United Methodist congregation. The church is active in the age-old customs of Sunday school conventions, fifth Sunday gatherings, and the church is most faithful in paying its apportionments to the mission of the denomination and the annual conference. At meal times, one will find the traditional Choctaw foods of banaha, poshofa, pork dishes, and the more contemporary fry bread.

This historic Choctaw church is certainly one that believes it is in mission and ministry in the life of their community and the denomination. If an outsider watched and observed, they might not agree that this church is a vital congregation. However, through the lens of the community and tribal peoples, it certainly is one. This particular church has been on a circuit for years. In the absence of the pastor who is serving one of the other two to three churches in that circuit, the church carries on. They know what to do to make the church work. They are effective in teaching Sunday school and in preaching. They have created their own structure of worship that fits into their own tribal culture. They love their church and they are serious about their spirituality that is lived out through that church.

One of the many contributions OIMC has provided in its 180-year history is the leadership it has provided to the denomination, especially in the last thirty to forty years. Native Americans not only serve on general agency staff, but also provide leadership to churches throughout the denomination in new church starts. OIMC is proud of their work throughout the denomination; they not only provide pastoral leadership, but also lay leadership from a Native American perspective. The United Methodist Church is unique in that we have one of the largest Native American populations of any mainline Protestant denomination, and because of our structure, OIMC is truly a conference led by indigenous people. The United Methodist Church prides itself on being a global church and one of the unique factors we have is that Native Americans have stayed in the denomination even though they were evangelized before their removal. They have an important cultural and historical perspective

Jalisa Ross, an Oklahoma University graduate, reflects on the contributions of the conference.

The Oklahoma Indian Missionary Conference is representative of many tribes, languages, and cultures. OIMC offers the denomination a very culturally diverse conference. Ross believes that, through the OIMC, Native Americans help contribute to the cultural diversity within our denomination. When outsiders look at OIMC they see it as the "Indian Conference," but in reality OIMC is made up of many Native American nations and tribes, each with their own language, culture, traditions, and ways of worshiping. OIMC enhances our denomination with its many facets of worship because it is so culturally diverse. The young adults are the ones in the conference who are pushing their elders to preserve the languages of their native tribes as well as some of their traditions and spiritual customs.

Native American young people were forced into Native American boarding schools by the U.S. government and it was drilled into them to just blend in; forget your language, traditions, culture, and customs. Ross says her generation, as well as her mother's, are trying to preserve as many of their traditions and as much of their culture as possible. It is important for young people to be able to pass on the languages to the younger children through their elders before they are completely lost. The churches are where this is taking place. The language, Bibles, tribal hymns, and spiritual customs are combined in the churches in addition to a traditional United Methodist worship experience.

"So, when we talk about the global nature of the church," Ross says, "it is important to recognize we are gifted with the diverse nations within this missionary conference. OIMC is a giving conference. Outsiders when coming to OIMC should know that hospitality is very important to us. Please come to our annual conference under the trees and experience our radical hospitality. We have received so we endeavor to give back."

Ross served as an intern for the Church Center for the United Nations and was able to be a part of the Permanent Forum for Indigenous People. The United Methodist Church had an opportunity to be on the floor of the United Nations, and Jalisa was able to represent indigenous people there.

IN CONVERSATION

to offer to The United Methodist Church in spite of how the church and the government has treated them. OIMC and Native Americans help to make the United Methodist church more diverse and are a needed presence in the UMC.

OIMC receives three to four calls a year from annual conferences looking for leadership to help them start ministries. They assist conferences in other ways such as conducting lay speaking classes from a Native American perspective and

unique leadership development training for Native American ministries and churches throughout the United States.

We are very proud of our partnership with the Oklahoma Conference; when disasters strike throughout Oklahoma, we share team resources. When the Oklahoma Conference closes a church, they reach out to us to see if a new native church starting out wants it. We are blessed by this partnership.

According to the statistics from the most recent Native American Sunday, Native Americans are a growing population within the denomination and OIMC has contributed to that by assisting conferences with leadership development. Another way growth is shown is the number of young adults who are participating in church. They have pushed OIMC leadership to embrace language and culture into the life of the ministries. An important emphasis has been service to community, as well as sharing their culture and language and putting Native American spirituality into practice.

Challenges are always what the conference is able to pay the lay leadership, licensed and unlicensed, and elders. OIMC is still operating below the poverty line and yet because they pay everyone the same there is a real commitment on the part of those who are in service; they want to be there in ministry and service to serve their own people. Their love of God and the sacrifice their leadership is willing to make is impressive.

OIMC continues to be in ministry with Native Americans from some thirty-nine nations in Oklahoma and bordering states. The pernicious effects of poverty and centuries of oppression are real, but the vibrant spirits and the dedicated people of faith in these congregations have something to offer the whole United Methodist Church as well as the whole of Christianity.

The previous chapter about the Alaska Missionary Conference included a petition from Alaska passed at General Conference 2016 that allows a missionary conference to become a missionary district under the supervision of the geographic annual conference in which it falls.

Petition Number: 60529-MH-¶415.4-G; . . .
The mission district may be organized in the same manner and have the same rights and powers as any district. Rationale: In some jurisdictions—Southeastern and Western—there are missionary con-

ferences that might better be organized as districts; this change will make that possible without removing the mission status of such entities. What the full implication is of being a mission district would be left to the annual conferences to determine.

The final line of this petition leaves it up to the annual conferences to determine the implications of such a change. If the option of becoming a missionary district had been in place when Native Americans in Oklahoma were trying to gain autonomy, they might not have been allowed to oversee their own churches, ordain their own clergy, or own their own property.

Conclusion

Methodist missions with black slaves, Native Americans, Norwegians, Germans, Alaskans, Appalachians, and others have come in waves, as spiritual needs based on the realities of demographics, politics, and economics emerge among peoples in new contexts and challenging times. As we have seen, some missions and missionary conferences faded into history as language, cultural, and economic barriers decreased with each generation.

Yet, three missionary conferences survive to this day. Alaska works in partnership with the Pacific Northwest Annual Conference, and may lean toward becoming a missionary district with them in the future. Red Bird clergy and congregations have occasionally moved back and forth between Red Bird and the Kentucky Annual Conference, and Red Bird may one day become more integrated into the larger geographic entity.

Leaders of the Oklahoma Indian Missionary Conference have no plans to change the conference's status, but sometimes the larger church makes decisions without understanding its own history. On the face of it, OIMC cannot really afford its ministries, but The United Methodist Church cannot afford to live without the OIMC.

Endnotes

1. "Indian Removal: 1814–1858," *Judgment Day*, PBS, accessed February 23, 2016, www.pbs.org/wgbh/aia/part4/4p2959.html.

2. Homer Noley, *First White Frost: Native Americans and United Methodism* (Nashville: Abingdon Press, 1991), 127.

3. Jerry R. Desmond, *Georgia's Rome: A Brief History* (Charleston, SC: The History Press, 2008), accessed February 23, 2016, https://books.google.com/books?id=tqkqwyu3uP0C&pg=PA24&lpg=PA24&dq=Georgia%27s+Rome:+A+Brief+History+22,000+cattle&source=bl&ots=rBrnB3LXI7&sig=cnIWnTuL-jxNrkKv1sWHd0Q8RwA&hl=en&sa=X&ved=0ahUKEwikwvHU3o7LAhUEXD4KHR0gB-wQ6AEIHDAA#v=onepage&q=Georgia's%20Rome%3A%20A%20Brief%20History%2022%2C000%20cattle&f=false.

4. David Williams, *The Georgia Gold Rush: Twenty-Niners, Cherokees, and Gold Fever* (Columbia: University of South Carolina Press, 1994), accessed February 23, 2016, https://books.google.com/books?id=wnaGLgY_fZcC&dq=Georgia+discovered+gold+cherokee&hl=en&sa=X&ved=0ahUKEwiS1NfE4o7LAhUFcj4KHeVwB-kQ6AEIPDAC.

5. Vicki Rozema, *Voices from the Trail of Tears* (Winston-Salem, NC: John F. Blair, Publisher, 2003), accessed February 23, 2016, https://books.google.com/books?id=Y7zgcpmg8vcC&pg=PA51&lpg=PA51&dq=methodist+at+the+trail+of+tears&source=bl&ots=jz665yGNRK&sig=lel_owq9MDFMpxoURcp6UDswBa0&hl=en&sa=X&ved=0ahUKEwji9uTc7I7LAhWEMyYKHRzCCWsQ6AEIOzAF#v=onepage&q=methodist%20at%20the%20trail%20of%20tears&f=false.

6. Will Chavez, "Historic Profile: Missionaries Stood with Cherokees to Fight Removal," *Cherokee Phoenix*, August 21, 2012, www.cherokeephoenix.org/Article/Index/6541.

7. "Treaty of New Echota," Cherokee Nation, accessed August 20, 2016, www.cherokee.org/AboutTheNation/History/TrailofTears/TreatyofNewEchota.aspx.

8. "Gathering at Horseshoe Bend Remembers and Looks to Future of Reconciliation, Repentance and Affirmation," North Alabama Conference of The United Methodist Church, November 19, 2014, www.umcna.org/postdetail/492074.

9. "James K. Polk: Life in Brief," Miller Center of the University of Virginia, accessed February 18, 2016, http://millercenter.org/president/biography/polk-life-in-brief.

10. Noley, *First White Frost*, 164.

11. Ibid., 161.

12. Francis Paul Prucha, *American Indian Policy in Crisis: Christian Reformers and the Indian, 1865–1900* (Norman: University of Oklahoma Press, 2014), 19, https://books.google.com/books?id=vMhcAwAAQBAJ&pg=PA19&lpg=PA19&dq=the+hitherto+untried+policy+in+connection+with+Indians&source=bl&ots=GeQgsXOXlM&sig=Sld26ebCnxtZuFafItppcps_6Hs&hl=en&sa=X&ved=0ahUKEwjzgZD5iIXOAhVDFz4KHSTmA38Q6AEIHjAA#v=onepage&q=the%20hitherto%20untried%20policy%20in%20connection%20with%20Indians&f=false.

13. Kevin Abing, "Directors of the Bureau of Catholic Indian Missions," Marquette University Archives, 1994, http://studylib.net/doc/8185834/directors-of-the-bureau-of-catholic-indian-missions.

14. Ibid.

15. Francis Paul Prucha, *American Indian Policy in Crisis*, 58.

16. Martha Stewart, "Oklahoma Indian Missionary Conference," *The Chronicles of Oklahoma* (Oklahoma Historical Society, 1941), 332, accessed July 23, 2016, http://digital.library.okstate.edu/Chronicles/v040/v040p330.pdf.

17. "Methodists," Oklahoma Historical Society website, accessed July 23, 2016, http://www.okhistory.org/publications/enc/entry.php?entry=ME020.

18. Ibid.

19. The Rev. Dr. David Wilson OIMC superintendent, telephone interview with author, February 2016.

20. Ronald J. Bacigal, "Judicial Reflections Upon the 1973 Uprising at Wounded Knee," University of Richmond, UR Scholarship Repository, 1998, http://scholarship.richmond.edu/cgi/viewcontent.cgi?article=1165&context=law-faculty-publications.

21. Emily Chertoff, "Occupy Wounded Knee: A 71-Day Siege and a Forgotten Civil Rights Movement," *The Atlantic*, October 23, 2012, www.theatlantic.com/national/archive/2012/10/occupy-wounded-knee-a-71-day-siege-and-a-forgotten-civil-rights-movement/263998.

22. The Rev. Dr. David Wilson OIMC superintendent, telephone interview with author, February 2016.

23. "Lilly Fawn White: US-2 Class 2008–2010," General Board of Global Ministries, accessed February 24, 2016, www.umcmission.org/Get-Involved/Generation-Transformation/Global-Mission-Fellows/Alumni/Testimonials/lily-fawn-white.

24. David Dodman, "In Alaska, Songs from Oklahoma," KNOM Mission, accessed February 24, 2016, www.knom.org/wp/blog/2013/11/15/in-alaska-songs-from-oklahoma.

25. Anita Phillips, executive director of The United Methodist Church Native American Comprehensive Plan, telephone interview with author, February 2016.

26. Jalisa Ross, OIMC young adult, telephone interview with Deborah Bass, April 2016.

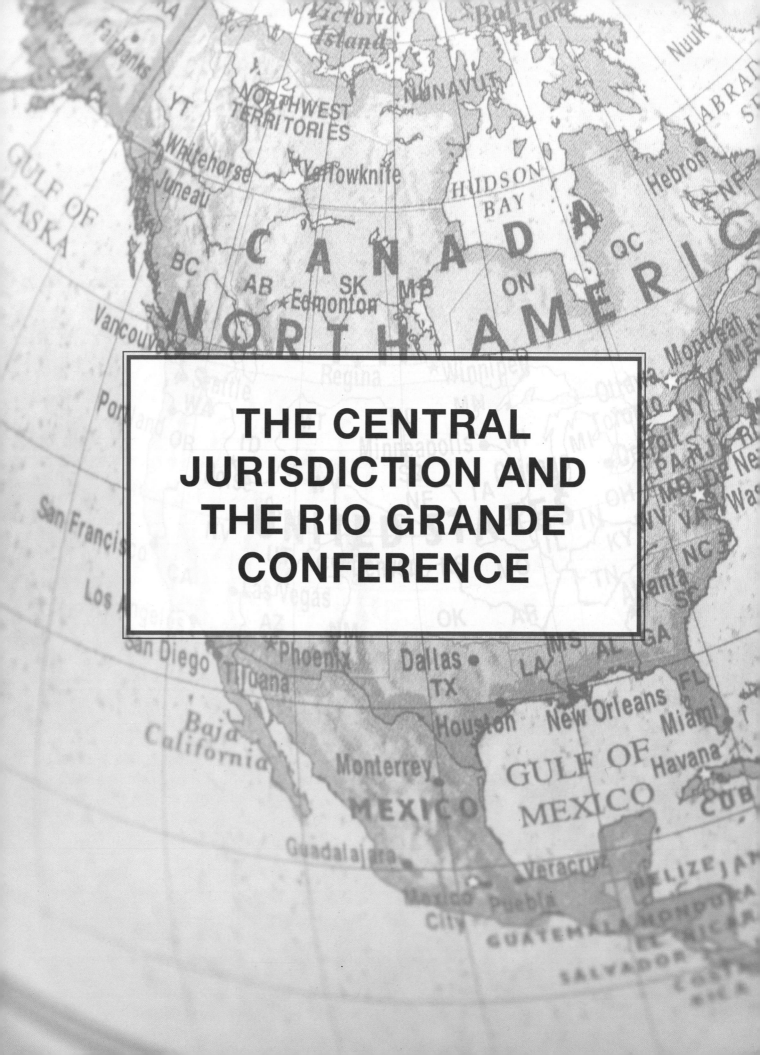

THE CENTRAL JURISDICTION AND THE RIO GRANDE CONFERENCE

CHAPTER 7

These three missionary conferences of the United Methodist Church we have studied thus far cannot be understood without talking about two church structures that are no longer in existence, the Central Jurisdiction and the Rio Grande Conference. The Central Jurisdiction was the segregated jurisdiction from 1939 to 1968. The Rio Grande Conference was the Spanish-language conference, which covered Texas and New Mexico until 2014 when its member churches transferred to the geographical conferences where they are located.[1]

In many ways, both met the criteria for being missionary conferences but neither was designated as such. Both covered vast amounts of territory, and both were comprised of people who had experienced the cultural and financial consequences of racism in the United States. For both groups, the church provided comfort and support, as well as domination and exploitation.

Early Methodism emphasized religious experience more than doctrine so it had an egalitarian feel to it; nonetheless, black members were not accorded equal footing. Harry Hoosier and Richard Allen were both at the Christmas Conference of 1784 but were not allowed to vote.[2] Hoosier was described as the "best preacher in the world" by Thomas Coke but was never allowed

to be ordained, despite a petition signed by nineteen ministers that was submitted to the Philadelphia conference in 1805 asking that Harry Hoosier be ordained. Richard Allen went on to reject mistreatment from white Methodists by forming the African Methodist Episcopal Church.[3]

We remember that John Wesley condemned slavery to his dying day in 1791, but the colonies and Christianity were steeped in race ideology, long before Wesley was born.

W.E.B. DuBois, iconic Pan-African scholar (1868–1963), collected and analyzed historic citations of policies, statements, and beliefs about people of African descent and religion in his 1903 report at an Atlanta University conference, "The Negro Church."[4] He noted that in early America, British schools for both black and Native American slaves were designed to convert them to Christianity, but revolts by slaves led to doubts about educating slaves among the ruling classes, as this example from DuBois's report reveals. At the time, Elias Neau served as "Schoolmaster and Catechist of the Negroes & Indians in New York."

In 1712 the Negroes in New York conspired to destroy all the English, which greatly discouraged the work of their instruction. The conspiracy was defeated, and many Negroes taken and executed.

Mr. Neau's school was blamed as the main occasion of the barbarous plot; two of Mr. Neau's students were charged with the plot; one was cleared and the other was proved to have been in the conspiracy. . . . In a short time, the cry against the instruction of the Negroes subsided: the governor visited and recommended the school. . . . [eventually,] the rector, church wardens, and vestry of Trinity Church in New York city requested another catechist, "there being about 1,400 Negro and Indian slaves, a considerable number of whom had been instructed in the principles of Christianity by the late Mr. Neau, and had received baptism and were communicants in their church. The society complied with this request and sent over the Rev. Mr. Colgan in 1726, who conducted the school with success." [5]

By the late 1700s, slavery was ensconced in the newly formed United States. The Founding Fathers knew that slavery was a violation of basic human freedoms they claimed for themselves, but they refused to write freedom for all into the U.S. Constitution. Thomas Jefferson never condemned slavery. George Washington was the only slave-holding Founding Father to free his slaves, and only through his will after his death and the death of his wife, Martha.[6] Still, attitudes began to shift.

Although slavery was legal in every Northern state at the beginning of the American Revolution, its economic impact was marginal. As a result, Northern Founders were freer to explore the libertarian dimensions of Revolutionary ideology. The experience of [Benjamin] Franklin was in many ways typical of the evolving attitudes of Northern Founders toward slavery. Although enmeshed in the slave system for much of his life, Franklin eventually came to believe that slavery ought to be abolished gradually and legally. Franklin himself had owned slaves, run ads in his *Pennsylvania Gazette* to secure the return of fugitive slaves, and

defended the honour of slaveholding revolutionaries. By 1781, however, Franklin had divested himself of slaves, and shortly thereafter he became the president of the Pennsylvania Abolition Society. He also went further than most of his contemporaries by signing a petition to the First Federal Congress in 1790 for the abolition of slavery and the slave trade.[7]

Many Methodist preachers took Wesley's antislavery message to heart and preached against the enslavement of any person. Pushback from Virginia plantation owners took a toll, and Francis Asbury, bishop of the Methodist Episcopal Church, wrote a letter telling ministers to preach TO the slaves, not against slavery. Slave owners and leading Methodists like William Capers, editor of the *Southern Christian Advocate*, argued that slavery "tended to the salvation of Negroes."[8] This shift used the excuse of soul saving to leave the "execrable" (Wesley's word) institution of slavery in place, thus bolstering the ideology of white supremacy and driving slavery and genocide.

The Central Jurisdiction

After the Civil War, white Methodist conflicts continued between Northern and Southern Methodists. For many decades interminable meetings among the various Methodist denominations explored a union. The debates included the role of bishops, the power of the General Conference, and what was described as "The Negro Problem." (Although this phrase seems distorted to most of us today—shifting the blame for racism to the victims—it was commonly used into the 1960s.) The denominations avidly discussed these issues—all without the input of African Americans—until a 1916 meeting in Evanston, Illinois. Although this meeting was not one of the "official" meetings about the union, it finally included speeches by representatives of the African Methodist Episcopal Church (AME), AME Zion, black Methodists in the MEC, as well as representatives of the Christian Methodist Episcopal (CME) churches. (CME is the denomination that was set up for black Methodists in the South, originally called "Colored Methodist Episcopal" churches). On some level, everyone participating wanted to be a good Christian, but the tenor of the conversation was always framed by white supremacist attitudes like "helping the lesser races" and the "uplifting of the race," as voiced by Booker T. Washington in that time. In the end, black leaders had to persuade white Methodists to pursue a union that did not include completely removing black people and their churches from the Methodist Episcopal Church. It took some doing.

Robert E. Jones, a church leader who went on to become a bishop in 1920, took on the task of persuading white Methodist men to give black Methodists something more than the Southern solution of setting them completely aside, and something less than full equality. Blake Renfro, in his thesis for Louisiana State University, describes Robert E. Jones as the editor of the *Southwestern Christian Advocate*, a black man whose family had stayed in the MEC throughout difficult times. Jones argued in 1917:

> To whites fearful of black representation in the General Conference, Jones explained that in the MEC "the white membership as compared to the Negro is nine to one and there is no chance for Negro domination or intimidation." After all, he surmised blacks and whites already maintained essentially separate affairs. "He [the Negro] has his separate churches, his separate Conferences, and the only points of contact are on the general committees and at the General Conference. To us who live in the South this point of contact does not alarm." With the approval of whites, black Methodist leaders could oversee their fellow African Americans, without compromising white control of the General Conference. Like Booker

Washington's political strategy, Robert E. Jones' proposal for Methodist unification promoted black leadership, but did so without threatening white dominance. Jones ultimately accepted segregation, but asked for black annual conferences, which had already voluntarily segregated, to maintain "absolutely equal in every regard to any other areas or districts in the church." Interracial contact would take place "in the General Conference, where we [African Americans] are to be on absolutely equal footing, to vote and to be voted for. From this upper chamber, we would each go down to our task to which we are related and adapted." As such, whites and blacks would never have to worship together in the local parish. And, the minimal black representation in the General Conference would never achieve enough power to trump white dominance. [9]

Jones bluntly stated his idea of a reunited Methodism. "Now I state in one sentence the program: The largest possible contact of the Negro with the white man with the largest possible independence of the Negro." [10]

Thus the Central Jurisdiction was formed.

Methodist women, both North and South, had resisted the segregated jurisdiction and were working toward mutual understanding, but the power structures of sex, race, and class were daunting.

> In 1920, two white members of the MECS [Methodist Episcopal Church, South] Women's Missionary Council (WMC) met with the leadership of the National Association of Colored Women (NACW), believing that hearts and attitudes could be changed through personal contact. Southern white women continued to work with and for black women through the WMC and the Commission on Interracial Cooperation (CIC). Focusing on the social sphere where they had some degree of power, white

women worked to provide childcare, improve skills and working conditions of domestic workers and increase educational opportunities for black women, so they could "aspire to larger usefulness." In the 1930's MECS women opposed the formation of the Central Jurisdiction in the merger with the MEC and the Protestant Church (MPC), believing that the segregated structure contradicted the relational ethic of Jesus' teaching. In hopes of defeating the plan, women succeeded in electing fifty-four female delegates to the 1938 MECS General Conference when the merger was considered, but white male voices promoting racial separation prevailed.[11]

Could the black churches have been a missionary conference? Distance was no real obstacle, as the Norwegian, Spanish, Japanese, German, and Chinese missions covered multiple states. *The Book of Discipline* says, "A conference is a missionary conference because of its particular mission opportunities, its limited membership and resources, its unique leadership requirements, its strategic regional or language considerations and ministerial needs."[12]

Black church leaders in search of a way to maintain a place in the newly forming Methodist Episcopal Church were looking for parity—despite the need to hold the hands of whites that feared anything but white control. They made their goal a jurisdiction that could be independent and run by black leaders, who would go to General Conference and be on equal footing—albeit in the minority—with white delegates.

The racially segregated Central Jurisdiction was approved by churches in the North and South in 1939, despite the protests of some. This segregation lasted for thirty years until the next union, between the Methodist Church and the Evangelical United Brethren (EUB), in 1968. The 1960s were a time of national turmoil. One hundred

years after emancipation from slavery, African Americans were still subject to oppression, discrimination, and KKK terrorism. The Rev. Dr. Martin Luther King Jr. and so many others, including many Methodists, marched and rallied and went to prison fighting for justice, voting rights, and the elimination of Jim Crow laws.

In that moment, the proposed union of the Methodist and EUB denominations brought the segregated jurisdiction into sharp focus. It had to go. As part of the merger, efforts were made to maintain the leadership and power bases of black Methodist churches, but there was little understanding by whites that institutions, churches, communities, and organizational structures formed under the Central Jurisdiction mattered, let alone black leadership. There was an attitude that African Americans had to work their way to the top of the white power structure rather than be brought in as people who had made a way out of no way.

When the Gulfside Assembly's retreat center on the coast of Mississippi was washed away by Hurricane Katrina in 2005, few whites knew that a large portion of Central Jurisdiction history was washed away with it; buildings, documents, photos, memories were gone.

Today, virtually all churches are struggling for members and money, but African Americans were hit hardest by the great recession in 2008 brought on by the deregulation of banks and the mortgage industry.

The black leaders who were fighting for a place in the emerging Methodist Church knew that economics counted. They reminded the white decision makers that, in 1896, the "colored conferences" had increased their annual apportionments and, by 1916, the African American Washington and Delaware Annual Conferences were self-sustaining. They pointed out that Negro MEC missionary offerings were greater than the AME, AMEZ, and Colored MEC (South) combined. [13]

Although Booker T. Washington's "lifting of the races" and black Methodists' appropriation of his way of thinking sounds demeaning when compared to later calls for racial equality by W.E.B. DuBois, Martin Luther King Jr., and other black equality strategists, economic and cultural solidarity in minority communities was and is a means to address systems of white privilege that demoralize and disintegrate black communities —without waiting for whites to change.

To merge or not to merge and on what terms were critical questions for members of the Central Jurisdiction in those days, as race relations are today.

What are the questions we, as Methodists, need to be asking about potential mergers of conferences today? What are the potential impacts of the possible incorporations of the Alaska United Methodist Conference and the Red Bird Missionary Conference into existing conferences? Will leaders in the Oklahoma Indian Missionary Conference feel pressure to be something other than a missionary conference? Will they continue in their commitment to self-determination and the assignment and training of the native pastors who serve OIMC churches? Will cost factors create pressure to merge into the Oklahoma Conference, as it did for the Rio Grande Conference?

The Rio Grande Conference

The Rio Grande Annual Conference was another conference that had some of the characteristics of a missionary conference, but was organized as a full annual conference for many years. It was disbanded in 2014 and absorbed into annual conferences in Texas and New Mexico as a cost-saving effort and a reflection of growing Spanish-language ministries in the conferences of the South Central Jurisdiction.

Rio Grande was a language conference, and as was true of many of the language conferences of the past, it was common for language conferences (German, Norwegian, Japanese, for example) to eventually merge into English-speaking conferences after a couple of generations had elapsed, when most of these folks spoke English. But each group still had its own history. Japanese Methodists have stories of internment during World War II. Chinese churches often use Chinese because of the waves of immigrants from China who continue to come to the United States. Many Northern European immigrants found their way to ethnic enclaves in big cities or became the driving force in little towns in the Midwest. They learned English and believed in the American "melting pot," but many of these communities still hold ethnic festivals each year.

The distinction between Methodist conferences made up of people of European descent and the Hispanic Rio Grande Conference was the ideology of Manifest Destiny. Native and Hispanic peoples were, and continue to be, primary targets of Manifest Destiny. [14] The ideology that the United States is a country founded on God, a Christian nation, is Manifest Destiny at work. Manifest Destiny requires that everyone must become a Christian or be pushed out (or worse).

Underneath the rejection and condemnation of others is the belief that European Americans own and deserve this country because God gave it to Anglo Protestants.

This idea of "otherness" was amplified by early Protestants in Texas because Texas itself was a foreign country in the early years. It first belonged to Native Americans, then Spain, France, and Mexico; then became its own country before becoming a U.S. state—and then a Confederate State. The population was sparse and often transient.

> In 1800, fewer than 5,000 colonists clustered around San Antonio, Goliad, and Nacogdoches. The Mexican War of Independence from Spain (1810–21) took a further toll, and by 1821 only two Franciscan friars and some 2,500 Mexicans remained in Texas. . . . by 1829 there were no Catholic bishops in all of Texas. [15]

The vacuum left by the Spaniards was being filled by Americans surging west, which prompted more wars with both Comanche and Cherokees in Texas in the mid-1800s.

When the Civil War pushed armed Texans to leave the area to fight Yankees, Comanche warriors used the opportunity (when the U.S. Army was not present) to push settlers back, but not for long. When the war ended, the U.S. soldiers returned to the area to protect the frontier. Epidemics of cholera and small pox broke out. The Comanche were defeated, and then restricted to a reservation in Oklahoma.

The few Methodists that made it as far west as Texas in the early to mid-1800s did not know the Spanish language, so they focused their mission efforts on other settlers, while trying to survive—and debated the issue of slavery.

Macum Phelon's *A History of Early Methodists in Texas, 1817–1866*, published by Cokesbury Press in 1924, confirms that Spanish speakers were not on the minds of Methodists. [16] This collection of papers and firsthand accounts also reveals that Methodists in Texas were embroiled in aggressive and sometimes violent conflicts between those allied with the Southern churches and the Northern churches.

In 1844, when the denomination split between South and North, rumors of plots and secret groups of Northern Methodist abolitionists in Texas spread quickly. When a letter addressed to the MEC pastor Rev. Bewley surfaced implicating him as an abolitionist, he was brought to court. He did not pay bail, and as he was being taken to the jailhouse, a mob of some three hundred took charge and hanged him. [17]

Another firsthand account shared in Phelon's book tells of a slave of high value who was whipped to death by an overseer. The local Methodist minister recommended that the overseer be charged with murder, but the owner decided legal action wasn't a good idea, because if the overseer left, he might not get the value of his slave back. [18] In the middle of the collection, Phelon includes an accounting of "property" in Texas, including the dollar value of its slave population:

> The year 1860 found both the State and the Church in a prosperous and growing condition. Texas had 604,251 people, by the Federal census, an increase of 391,623 during the previous decade, or 184.2 per cent. The increase during the war decade, or from 1860 to 1870, dropped to 35 per cent. Of the population in 1860, 136,853 were negro slaves, who had been "rendered for taxation" the previous year at a total valuation of $85,630,748, average value "per head" of $625,541. The slave wealth of the state overtopped that from any other source, even exceeding the value of land rendered for taxation, and being two and one-half times the value of all the horses and cattle put together. These figures are of interest as pointing to the sacrifice of wealth which the war was to entail upon Texas alone. And it is little wonder that, with so much property at stake, short work

was made of any "abolition" crusades whether political or ecclesiastical. (Figures from *Texas Almanac*, 1860.)[19]

This was the backdrop for the formation of mission to Spanish-speaking peoples in Texas and further west. Texas was incorporated into the United States as a slave state in 1845 after a war with Mexico (and just as Methodists were splitting). Mexico was an enemy, and anyone who spoke Spanish was suspected of being a sympathizer. The first federal census taken of Texas in 1850 counted more than 14,000 residents of Mexican descent.[20]

Methodists were present in Texas in 1815, through the preaching of circuit rider William Stevenson near Red River in East Texas. As the Methodist church grew, annual conferences were organized with little to no mission work directed at Spanish-speaking populations.[21] In fact, Protestantism was illegal in Texas under Spanish rule until Texas won its independence from Mexico in 1836, as a precursor to becoming a state a decade later.[22]

In 1836, when Texas acquired independence from Mexico, people of Mexican descent remained concentrated in settlements founded during the eighteenth century, namely Nacogdoches, San Antonio, Goliad, and Laredo.[23] It wasn't until after the Civil War that Methodists begin to turn their attention to Mexican Americans, mostly to identify them as the pagan "other" who needed to be saved—and oppressed.

The Rev. Alexander Sutherland, a missionary of MEC (South) working in Texas and northern Mexico, wrote in 1883: "Age on age of darkness, duplicity, and degradation have left them [Mexicans] so full of evil, so prone to evil, that the task of purification and elevation would be utterly hopeless, leaving out the divinity of the agency."[24]

Despite this attitude, in 1885, the Mexican Border Missionary Conference South became official.

Over time, the boundaries and names of this conference shifted (see Appendix A); at the time of the 1939 union between Methodists in the North and South, it became the Southwest Mexican Annual Conference for Texas and New Mexico, and, in 1948, it became known as the Rio Grande Annual Conference.[25] There was also an Annual Conference called Rio Grande Mission (1859–63), and then Rio Grande (1864–65), but it was populated by Anglos and merged into the Southwest Texas Annual Conference after the Civil War.

Mexican Americans in early Methodism faced an uphill battle, both within their communities and in their churches. Whole families and towns were structured around the Catholic faith and practice. Converting to Methodism was, in effect, like converting to both another religion and moving to a foreign country. Harassment and splits in families were real, but for many the appeal of the Methodist tent revivals and the more personal relationship with God they promised was stronger.

Mexican Americans found few allies among whites in Texas in those days, but they reached a form of peaceful coexistence where the number of outright attacks decreased until 1910, when Mexicans surged across the border seeking relief from the violence of the Mexican Revolution (1910–20).[26] Anglo Texans in the region reacted out of fear and, for the next ten years, raids and violence ensued between the two groups over land. Then, the onset of the Great Depression in 1929 brought a growing xenophobia, and Mexican Americans became a target. By the 1930s, a "repatriation" program forced many Mexicans—both U.S. citizens and undocumented immigrants—to return to Mexico.[27]

Today, the exclusion and rejection of Mexicans and Latinos in general continues, fed by Anglo fears and resulting in political exploitation. We see the imprisonment of children who cross the border,[28] deportation of the parents of children who have only known the United States as home, and political candidates saying, "They are bringing drugs, they are bringing crime, they are rapists."[29] Public disdain of U.S. citizens of Hispanic descent is serious and lethal. Demographics for poverty, incarceration, and discrimination are similar to those of African Americans.[30] And, in a contemporary version of slave labor, untold numbers of undocumented Hispanic immigrants work for almost nothing, and many who work are not paid at all.[31]

So why would Mexican Americans have chosen a predominantly Anglo denomination like the Methodist Church—and the Southern Methodist Church, at that? And why did they participate in the formation of the Rio Grande Conference and, prior to that, the Mexican Border Mission Conference, the Texas Mexican Mission, and the Western Mexican Mission?

Paul Barton, Tejano and Methodist native son, is associate professor of history of American Christianity and missiology and director of Hispanic church studies at the Seminary of the Southwest in Austin, Texas. In his book *Hispanic Methodists, Presbyterians and Baptists*, he does not mince words about the racism and economic exploitation faced by Tejanos (Mexican-American inhabitants of southern Texas).

Barton is also clear that, although adaptions and assimilations happened, Mexican Americans survived these changes. Not only did Methodists shape Tejanos, Tejanos shaped Methodism. In the process, the church became a place of preserving families, cultural identity, and even the

Tejanos's lives in a challenging and sometimes hostile world.

> Examining Protestantism as a vehicle for assimilation into mainstream American society tells only one side of the story of Hispanic Protestantism. While some degree of assimilation resulted from Protestant influence, los Protestantes continued to practice their Mexican-American culture within their religious communities. Indeed, congregational life enabled the maintenance of their Mexican-American culture. This is the case with the Rio Grande Annual Conference, whose ministry in northern Mexico, Texas, and New Mexico dates back over 100 years. . . . These congregations provided safe environments where los Protestantes could engage in cultural self-preservation.[32]

Barton points out that eventually, the bridge back to Catholicism was built through common work in the farmworkers justice movement. Emerging Catholic social justice values harmonized with a more relaxed approach to Methodist morality in a social context. Prohibitions against drinking, dancing, and gambling transformed into a concern for people with addictions, such as gambling.

Today, more people are becoming increasingly aware of how our own cultures influence the way we do things. They are learning to treasure the mestizo, or mixture, of cultures and influences within each of us, our church, and our country. At the same time, the dominant culture has not yet reckoned with the obliteration of whole swaths of people in the name of Manifest Destiny and presumed white superiority.

These are not just historical facts that have little to do with us today—or a form of whining about the mistakes people made in the past. A belief in Manifest Destiny and white superiority are the lifeblood that feeds the ongoing criminalization of people of color, the continuing dismissal of existing treaties about the tribal lands of Native American people, the ridicule of poor white people, and the rabid exploitation of our natural environment.

In a poignant "here I stand" kind of closing to his book, in 2006, Barton recounts the attempts to merge the Rio Grande Conference with other conferences in Texas, and how leaders in the Rio Grande stood their ground.

> . . . the Rio Grande Annual Conference considered merger with other Anglo-American dominant conferences in Texas and New Mexico. At the request of Rio Grande and Southwest Texas Annual Conferences, the Texas Methodist Planning Commission authorized in 1954 the inter-Conference Commission to study the relationship between the Rio Grande Annual Conference and other annual conferences in Texas and New Mexico. The commission offered several options to improve the Spanish-speaking work and develop closer cooperation between Anglo- and Mexican-American Methodists. One of the options included a merger of the Rio Grande Annual Conference with other conferences. The conference chose not to pursue the option of merger. The conference undertook its own self-study from 1965 to 1967, at the end of which it reaffirmed its status as a separate annual conference. The self-study settled any questions among the conference's members about the possibility of merging with other conferences. From that time onward, the conference has continually asserted its right to exist as a separate, language-based conference. Conference members have decided that the advantage of self-determination and continued fellowship among each other outweighs the disadvantages of extensive territorial boundaries, financial hardship and scarcity of resources. [33]

In 2014, less than a decade after Paul Barton wrote this testimony to his ancestors, the Rio Grande congregations merged into the geographic conferences in which the churches found themselves—whether in Texas or New Mexico. The largest number of Rio Grande congregations became part of the new Rio Texas Annual Conference, which was formed from the former Rio Grande and Southwest Texas Conferences (see Appendix A).

According to the Unification Plan produced by the Rio Texas Conference, the unification of the Rio Grande Annual Conference and the Southwest Texas Annual Conference was motivated by the desire to grow the kingdom of God. Unification was intended to position the new conference to reach out to more people, more diverse people and younger people. Today, the Rio Texas Conference continues to live into the vision of uniting peoples, vitalizing congregations, developing missional leaders, and transforming communities. Congregations continue in their faithfulness to the church and the various ways of reaching people through various outreach ministries. In some areas, particularly in the Lower Rio Grande Valley area, partnerships, fellowships, and joint ministry endeavors continue out of their beginnings prior to unification. As planned, unification has provided a common language and direction for all ministry levels within the Rio Texas Conference—local, district, and conference—to reach out to more people, more diverse people, and younger people.

Endnotes

1. "2013 Rio Grande Annual Conference," The United Methodist Church, accessed August 20, 2016, www.umc.org/who-we-are/2013-2013-rio-grande-annual-conference.

2. Stephen H. Webb, "Introducing Black Harry Hoosier: The History Behind Indiana's Namesake," *Indiana Magazine of History*, March 2002, https://scholarworks.iu.edu/journals/index.php/imh/article/view/11895/17497.

3. Ibid.

4. Dubois, W.E.B. "The Negro Church. Report of a Social Study Made under the Direction of Atlanta University; Together with the Proceedings of the Eighth Conference for the Study of the Negro Problems, held at Atlanta University, May 26th, 1903," electronic edition, *Documenting the American South*, accessed February 29, 2016, 13, http://docsouth.unc.edu/church/negrochurch/dubois.html.

5. Ibid.

6. "Ten Facts About Washington and Slavery," George Washington's Mount Vernon, accessed March 1, 2016, www.mountvernon.org/george-washington/slavery/ten-facts-about-washington-slavery.

7. Anthony Iccarino, "The Founding Fathers and Slavery," *Encyclopædia Britannica*, July 28, 2016, www.britannica.com/topic/The-Founding-Fathers-and-Slavery-1269536.

8. Donald G. Matthews, "The Methodist Mission to the Slaves, 1829–1844," *The Journal of American History* 51, no. 4 (March 1965): 615–31, www.jstor.org/stable/1889804?seq=1#page_scan_tab_contents.

9. Blake Barton Renfro, "The Reunification of American Methodism, 1916–1939: A Thesis," Louisiana State University, accessed February 29, 2016, 38, http://etd.lsu.edu/docs/available/etd-04292010-132837/unrestricted/renfro_thesis.pdf.

10. Ibid.

11. Jane Ellen Nickell, *We Shall Not Be Moved: Methodists Debate Race, Gender and Homosexuality* (Eugene, OR: Wipf & Stock Publishers, 2014), 143–44, https://books.google.com/books?id=HMsSBQAAQBAJ&pg=PA144&lpg=PA144&dq=methodist+women+reject+segregated+central+jurisdiction&source=bl&ots=dbGC3eQ3hw&sig=RpTzJP2jLHIWkdd9bHu8X61-ObY&hl=en&sa=X&ved=0ahUKEwihpqepsJ7LAhWB74MKHbOEBCEQ6AEIXzAJ#v=onepage&q=methodist%20women%20reject%20segregated%20central%20jurisdiction&f=false.

12. *The Book of Discipline of The United Methodist Church, 2012*, "The Missionary Conference: Definition" ¶585 (Nashville: Abingdon Press, 2012), 388.

13. Renfro, "The Reunification of American Methodism," 42.

14. Virgilio Elizondo, "Hispanic Theology and Popular Piety: From Interreligious Encounter to a New Ecumenicism," *CTSA Proceedings* 48 (1993), 5, www.virgilioelizondo.com/1/docs/Hispanic%20Theology%20and%20Popular%20Piety%20From%20Interreligious%20Encounter%20to%20a%20New%20Ecumenism2.pdf.

15. "Mexican Americans and Religion," Texas State Historical Association, accessed February 23, 2016, https://tshaonline.org/handbook/online/articles/pqmcf.

16. Born to David S. Phelan and Elizabeth Cail near Trenton, Tennessee, Macum Phelan (1874–1950) was raised by relatives in Waco, Texas, after the death of his parents. Phelan attended the University of Texas at Austin (UT) and taught for six years in McLennan County; in 1900 he bought the *Moody Courier* and sold it two years later. Phelan returned to UT to study ministry and was ordained in 1907. Phelan was faculty at Southwestern University and Southern Methodist University, while writing *History of Early Methodism in Texas, 1817–1866 (1924), History of Methodism in Texas: Expansion of Methodism in Texas, 1867–1902 (1937), and A Handbook of all Denominations.*

17. Macum Phelan, *A History of Early Methodism in Texas, 1817–1866* (Nashville: Cokesbury Press, 1924), accessed March 1, 2016, 439–60, https://archive.org/stream/MN5075ucmf_0/MN5075ucmf_0_djvu.txt.

18. Ibid., 411.

19. Ibid., 558.

20. Celeste Ray, volume editor, and Charles Reagan Wilson, general editor, "Mexicans," *The New Encyclopedia of Southern Culture: Ethnicity*, volume 6, (Winston-Salem, NC: University of North Carolina Press, 2007), 296. www.jstor.org/stable/10.5149/9781469616582_ray.

21. Olin Nah, "Texas," *Encyclopedia of World Methodism*, volume II (Nashville: United Methodist Publishing House, 1974), 2328.

22. "Methodist Church," Texas State Historical Association, accessed March 5, 2016, tshaonline.org/handbook/online/articles/imm01.

23. "Mexican Americans," Texas State Historical Association, accessed March 5, 2016, https://tshaonline.org/handbook/online/articles/pqmue.

24. Paul Barton, *Hispanic Methodists, Presbyterians and Baptists in Texas* (Austin: University of Texas Press, 2006), 39.

25. Ibid., 14.

26. Allan Englekirk and Marguerite Marín, "Mexican Americans," *Countries and Their Cultures*, accessed March 5, 2016, www.everyculture.com/multi/Le-Pa/Mexican-Americans.html.

27. "America's Forgotten History of Mexican-American 'Repatriation,'" hosted by Terry Gross, NPR *Fresh Air*, September 10, 2015, www.npr.org/2015/09/10/439114563/americas-forgotten-history-of-mexican-american-repatriation.

28. Swanson, Torres, Thompson, Blue, & Hernández, "A Year After Obama Declared a 'Humanitarian Situation' at the Border, Child Migration Continues," North American Congress on Latin America, August 27, 2015, https://nacla.org/news/2015/08/27/year-after-obama-declared-%E2%80%9Chumanitarian-situation%E2%80%9D-border-child-migration-continues.

29. Sophia Kerby "The Top 10 Most Startling Facts About People of Color and Criminal Justice in the United States" Center for American Progress, March 13, 2012, www.americanprogress.org/issues/race/news/2012/03/13/11351/the-top-10-most-startling-facts-about-people-of-color-and-criminal-justice-in-the-united-states.

30. "The Wage Gap, by Gender and Race," Info Please, accessed March 5, 2016, www.infoplease.com/ipa/A0882775.html.

31. Annette Bernhardt, Ruth Milkman, Nik Theodore, et al, "Broken Laws, Unprotected Workers: Violations of Employment Laws in America's Cities," National Employment Law Project, 2009, www.nelp.org/content/uploads/2015/03/BrokenLawsReport2009.pdf?nocdn=1.

32. Barton, *Hispanic Methodists, Presbyterians and Baptists in Texas*, 30.

33. Ibid., 161.

CONCLUSION

The aim of this study is to give an overview of the three missionary conferences in The United Methodist Church, the contexts out of which they grew, and their current engagements. What of the future? Broad-ranging conversations are taking place around this question. Going forward, Global Ministries and the missionary conferences are exploring the best operational and structural options for maximizing mission and ministry in these unique locations. These dialogues, different in each case, have begun and will take place throughout the 2017–20 quadrennium. The objective is mutuality in mission, partnership, and collaboration, which provides the heartbeat of all productive mission within the United Methodist connection.

The three missionary conferences have boundaries and histories that cross cultural and geographic lines. Their respective locations are unique: They range from the vastness of Alaska to rugged but small Red Bird to the State of Oklahoma with small overlaps into Texas and Kansas. They represent opportunities for mission and ministry with a diversity of people: From Alaska's widespread populations to the often isolated communities within Red Bird's Appalachian Mountain region to Oklahoma's large population of First Nation peoples.

It is my prayer that as you have read about our precursor denominations and our three missionary conferences, as well as the Central Jurisdiction and various language conferences, you have reflected on questions like, "Where do I come from?" "What harms have my ancestors experienced or inflicted because of their identity?" "What gifts have been received?" "What lives and souls have been lost or saved?"

These reflections are grounded in the life, death, and resurrection of Jesus. His land was occupied territory—and the occupiers were not above lining the road with thousands of crucified bodies if a rebellion surged.[1] Jesus walked the path of a truth teller and grace giver in those tumultuous times. He walked that path even unto death, knowing that those in power did not have the final say over his life. He was in God's hands.

In these times of global change, there is no higher calling than to walk the path that Jesus showed us. Love God and neighbor, serve those in need, challenge injustice, and walk humbly with God.

Endnotes

1. "Sources for the Three Slave Revolts," Internet Ancient History Sourcebook, Fordham University, accessed August 20, 2016, http://sourcebooks.fordham.edu/ancient/3slaverevolttexts.asp.

ABOUT THE AUTHOR

Author

J. Ann Craig is a lifelong United Methodist, born in Oklahoma, and raised in Missouri and Nebraska. Ann attended Nebraska Wesleyan University. She moved to Virginia after college to be a US-2 home missionary in campus ministry before she attended Yale Divinity School. After seminary, Ann served as a National Division executive for the mission projects founded by women of the church, and then served United Methodist Women as the executive for Spiritual and Theological Development for seventeen years where she oversaw the annual spiritual growth study, organized retreats, and trained conference officers.

In 2007, Ann became the first director of religion at the Gay and Lesbian Alliance Against Defamation (GLAAD). After GLAAD, Ann set up her own business and directed the communications campaign for the Love Your Neighbor Coalition at General Conference, 2012, and worked as a consultant in 2016. Currently, Ann is working with the Fellowship Global in Africa to support progressive clergy who are becoming more inclusive in the name of religion.

Special Contributor

Deborah E. Bass, is the former deputy general secretary for the General Board of Global Ministries for Administration. Prior to moving to Administration she was an associate general secretary for Community Ministries and Congregational Development where she worked as Global Ministries' team leader for liaison relationships with the missionary conferences, a role she served in the former National Division.

Now retired, Deborah resides in Compton, California, where she lives with her ninety-eight-year-old mother and assists her with their urban garden.

APPENDIX A:
Denominational Merger Charts

The charts in this appendix show the mergers that led to the creation of the following conferences in The United Methodist Church. They were originally prepared in 1968 for *The Encyclopedia of World Methodism* by Albea Godbold and John H. Ness Jr. and continue to be updated periodically.[1]

The following is a list of the abbreviations used:

- MEC: Methodist Episcopal Church
- MC Methodist (1866–77)
- M: Methodist (1939–68)
- UM: United Methodist Church

- MES: Methodist Episcopal, South
- MP: Methodist Protestant Church
- UB: United Brethren Church
- EUB: Evangelical United Brethren

The Methodist Protestant Church and the secessionist Methodist Church (1866–77) afford incomplete and sometimes conflicting data. However, those MP conferences in the north and west who adhered to the Methodist Church are marked @. Asterisks (*) denote African-American annual conferences.

Alaska
The following chart shows the flow of the Alaska conference's status in The United Methodist Church. Whereas some conferences have experienced complicated mergers, or overlapping conferences based on race, culture, and language, Alaska's history of conference identifications flows fairly simply from founding and then through mergers with slight changes in name.

Denom.	Conference	Dates	Location	How Formed	Conclusion
ME	Alaska Mission	1904–24	AK	New work	Absorbed by Puget Sound
M	Alaska Mission	1939–60	AK	Division of Pacific Northwest	Superseded by Alaska Mission Conference
M	Alaska Mission Conference	1961–68	AK	Superseded Alaska Mission	Continued in UM
UM	Alaska Mission Conference	1968–	AK	Superseded Alaska Mission Conference M	

Red Bird (Kentucky)

Denom.	Conference	Dates	Location	How Formed	Conclusion
ME	Western	1796–1812	KY, TN, OH, etc.	Original Conference	Divided Tennessee, Ohio
MES	Kentucky	1845–1939	KY	Superseded Kentucky ME	Continued in M
MES	Memphis	1845–1939	Western KY, Western TN	Superseded Memphis ME	Continued in M
MES	Louisville	1846–1939	Central KY	Division of Kentucky	Continued in M
MES	Western Virginia	1850–1939	Eastern KY	New work	Merged 1939
MP	Tennessee	1834–1939	KY, TN	Secession from ME	Merged 1939
MP	@Ohio	1830–46	KY, OH	Secession from ME	Ceded to Tennessee?
MP	Kentucky	1871–1939	KY	Division of Tennessee	Merged 1939
MP	West Tennessee	1854–87	KY, TN	Division of Tennessee	Superseded by Tennessee & Kentucky
MP	Virginia	1880–1939	KY, VA	New work	Merged 1939
M	Kentucky	1939–68	Eastern KY	Superseded Kentucky MES	Continued in UM
M	*Lexington	1939–64	KY, IN, OH, IL, MI	Superseded *Lexington ME	Superseded by *Tennessee-Kentucky
M	Louisville	1939–68	Central KY	Superseded Louisville MES	Continued in UM
M	Memphis	1939–68	Western KY, TN	Superseded Memphis MES	Continued in UM
M	*Tennessee-Kentucky	1965–68	KY, TN	Superseded Parts of *Lexington, *East Tennessee & *Tennessee	Merged 1968

Denom.	Conference	Dates	Location	How Formed	Conclusion
UB	Indiana	1833–50	KY, IN	New work	Superseded by Kentucky Mission
UB	Kentucky Mission	1850–1904	Eastern KY	Division of Indiana	Superseded by Kentucky
UB	Kentucky	1905–21	Eastern KY	Division of Indiana	Merged with Tennessee
UB	Lower Wabash	1897–1901	Northern KY, Southern IN	New work?	Superseded by Kentucky
UB	Miami	1897–1946	Northern KY, OH	New work?	Continued in EUB
UB	Ohio German	1865–1930	Northern KY, OH, etc.	New work	Disappeared
UB	Southern Indiana	1897–1901	Northern KY, Southern IN	Superseded Lower Wabash	Superseded by Kentucky
UB	Tennessee	1921–46	KY, TN	Merger Kentucky & Tennessee	Continued in EUB
EUB	Tennessee	1946–55	KY, TN	Superseded Tennessee UB	Divided into Tennessee & Kentucky
EUB	Kentucky	1955–68	KY	Division of Tennessee	Part continued in UM as Red Bird Mission
UM	Kentucky	1968–	Eastern KY	Superseded Kentucky M	
UM	Louisville	1968–96	Central KY	Superseded Louisville M	Merged with Kentucky
UM	Memphis	1968–	Western KY, TN	Superseded Memphis M	
UM	Red Bird Mission	1968–	Eastern KY	Superseded Red Bird Mission in Kentucky EUB	(Only unmerged former EUB work)

Oklahoma

Denom.	Conference	Dates	Location	How Formed	Conclusion
MES	Indian Mission Conference	1844–1906	Indian Territory	New work	Absorbed by Oklahoma
MES	Oklahoma	1906–10	OK	Superseded Indian Mission Conference	Divided into East Oklahoma & West Oklahoma
MES	Indian Mission	1918–39	OK	Reestablished by MES	Continued in M
MES	Oklahoma	1930–39	Oklahoma	Merger East Oklahoma & West Oklahoma	Continued in M
MES	West Oklahoma	1911–29	Western OK	Division of Oklahoma	Merged with East Oklahoma
MP	Chickasaw Mission	1896–1908	OK	New work	Absorbed by Oklahoma
MP	Fort Smith-Oklahoma	1916–39	OK	Superseded Oklahoma	Merged 1939
MP	Indian Mission	1892–1908	Indian Territory	New work	Absorbed by Oklahoma
MP	Oklahoma Mission	1896–1908	OK	Division of Fort Smith Mission	Superseded by Oklahoma

Denom.	Conference	Dates	Location	How Formed	Conclusion
MP	Oklahoma	1908–16	OK	Superseded Oklahoma Mission	Superseded by Fort Smith-Oklahoma
MP	Southwest Oklahoma Mission	1900–8	Southwest OK	New Indian work	Absorbed by Oklahoma
MP	Texhoma Mission	1928–32	OK, Northwest TX	Superseded Texas, Fort Smith-Oklahoma	Absorbed
M	East Oklahoma	1939–53	Eastern OK	Superseded parts of Oklahoma ME & Oklahoma MES	Merged with West Oklahoma as Oklahoma
M	Indian Mission	1939–58	OK	Superseded Indian Mission MES	Superseded by Oklahoma Indian Mission Conference
M	Oklahoma	1954–68	OK	Merger East Oklahoma & West Oklahoma	Continued in UM
M	Oklahoma Indian Mission Conference	1959–68	OK, KS, TX	Superseded Indian Mission	Continued in UM
M	*Southwest	1939–68	OK, AR	Superseded *Southwest ME	Continued in UM
M	West Oklahoma	1939–53	Western OK	Superseded parts of Oklahoma ME & Oklahoma MES	Merged with West Oklahoma as Oklahoma

Rio Grande | Rio Grande Annual Conference

Denom.	Conference	Dates	Location	How Formed	Conclusion
MES	Mexican Border Mission Conference	1885–1914	TX, Mexico	New work	Superseded by Mexican Border
MES	Mexican Border	1915–18	Western TX	Merger Mexican Border, Northwest Mexican Mission Conference	Superseded by Western Mexican Mission
MES	Texas Mexican Mission	1914–29	Southern TX	Partially superseded Mexican Border Mission Conference	Superceded by Texas Mexican
MES	Western Mexican Mission	1918–29	NM, AZ, TX, CA	Superseded Pacific Mexican Mission	Superceded Western Mexican
MES	Western Mexican	1930–39	NM, AZ, TX, CA	Superceded Western Mexican Mission	Merged into Latin American Provisional M
M	Latin American Provisional	1939–57	Western Jurisdiction, Part of Mexico	Merger of Latin American ME, Western Mexican MES	Merged with Anglo
M	Southwest Mexican	1939–48	NM, TX	Merger of Latin American Mission ME, Texas Mexican, Western Texas MES	Superseded by Rio Grande
M	Rio Grande	1948–68	NM, TX	Superseded Southwest Mexican	Continued in UM: In 2015 merged into Rio Texas and absorbed into NM and other Texas Conferences

Endnotes

1. All charts are by Albea Godbold and John H. Ness Jr., revised by Edwin Schell and Mark Shenise, "Table of United Methodist Church Annual Conferences 1796–2015," The General Commission on Archives and History, The United Methodist Church, revised January 2015, http://s3. amazonaws.com/gcah.org/Methodist_Table_Current_Edition.pdf.